DRAMA
IS OPTI NAL

11.30.06

DRAMA
IS OPTI☀NAL

A Guide For Teens

JUDEE AUSNOW

iUniverse, Inc.
New York Lincoln Shanghai

DRAMA IS OPTIONAL
A Guide For Teens

Copyright © 2007 by Judee Faye Ausnow

iUniverse books may be ordered through booksellers or by contacting:

iUniverse
2021 Pine Lake Road, Suite 100
Lincoln, NE 68512
www.iuniverse.com
1-800-Authors (1-800-288-4677)

ISBN: 978-0-595-42563-1 (pbk)
ISBN: 978-0-595-86892-6 (ebk)

Printed in the United States of America

To my granddaughters,

Jerri Cuerden and Delanie Ausnow.

I could only have imagined what a joy it would be

to be your grandmother.

You make my heart smile and I Love You Big!

G'Ma

CONTENTS

ACKNOWLEDGMENTS

I thank God for my wonderful family, who are always there to support me in everything I choose to do in life. A very special thanks to my sister, Janet Zornig, whose belief in me kept me going … Thanks Sis!

And, of course, thanks to all the great "teachers" in the field of self-improvement. Without their willingness to share their knowledge, and give of themselves to help others, I would not be the person I am today. I am grateful.

INTRODUCTION

What if … you found Aladdin's lamp and the Genie granted you three wishes. What would you wish for—after, of course, the million dollars and the car of your choice? Would you want to be a better student? Would you want to be more popular? Would you want to have better relationships with your family and friends? Would you want your body to be healthy and fit? Would you like all the *drama* in your life to be gone for good? As the title of this book suggests, drama is optional. According to Webster, "drama" is a series of emotional events, and "optional" means you have a choice to allow something or not.

As I scanned my computer for viruses the other day I thought about how easy it would be if we had a personal antivirus program, within our minds, to detect viruses that attack our thinking. If we could press a button and see what thoughts were causing us to feel jealous, hurt, and stressed, we could remove them from our consciousness. How easy it would be if we just created thoughts that would make us feel happy and make our lives work perfectly. The thing is … it *is* that easy!

Pretend your life is a book in progress and you are the author. Ask yourself what the completed chapters look like and how you want the next chapter to be. If you could create your life any way you choose, what would you change? What would you add to your life, and what would you take away from it? Look at the questions at the top of this page and really think about what you would like to create in your life. If the next chapter of your life could be any way you wanted it to be, if you truly were the author of your life—of your next experience—what would it be like?

Here's the secret to having the life you want: your life is created by your thoughts. When you ask people what they want in their lives, they usually start telling you what they don't want. What they don't realize is that we get exactly what we focus on—and focusing our attention on what we *don't* want just creates more of what we don't want in our lives. Most of us have a hard time describing what we *do* want because our attention is focused on what we don't want. What if we started thinking about what we *do* want—really thinking about what would make us happy, what would make *our hearts smile*—and started putting our attention on that? Ahh … what then?

Compare your life to a computer. It has been said that even in the most complicated computers there are only three components: the *hard drive*, the *operating system,* and the *programs*. Scientists have described life as a consciousness computer that also has only three components; *our physical world* is the hard drive, *our consciousness* is the operating system, *our thoughts* are the programs. You don't change the hard drive on your computer to create something new, you change the programs. It is the same in life. If you want to create something new for yourself, you don't have to change your physical world, you simply change your thoughts. Changing your thoughts literally changes the experience you create in your life because your thoughts create your feelings and emotions—and your feelings and emotions have the power to make you feel really, really good, or really, really bad.

I have been fortunate over the past twenty or so years to have studied with many great teachers in the field of self improvement. Through their seminars, books, and CD programs, I have learned valuable life lessons from people like Dr. Wayne W. Dyer, Marianne Williamson, Caroline Myss, don Miguel Ruiz, and Tony Robbins. The wisdom of these great teachers has given me the tools to create a life of peace, prosperity, and joy—and the passion to want that kind of life for others. I have learned that who we are is not what we do. You won't find a Ph.D. after my name; in fact the only designation you will see—work related—is real estate broker. I chose a career in real estate when I became a single parent thirty years ago so I could schedule my work time around my family time. I wanted to be available for the important things in life like keeping score at my daughter's basketball games and attending my son's football games. Who I am is much more than mother, grandmother, sister, aunt, and friend, but those are the designations I treasure most in my life. Please don't put this book down now because you just found out it was written by a grandmother. Remember that we learn from each other—and two of my greatest teachers are my teenaged granddaughters. Grandparents—and parents for that matter—have fallen down and gotten back up more times than we would like to admit in our lives, which, of course, creates the experiences we can use to write a book like this. The only way we learn anything is from experience, so pay attention to the experiences that feel good in your heart and allow them to create positive changes in your life.

The intent of this book is to offer you some tools to help you create your next chapter any way you choose. I have written this book for teens because I have two teenaged granddaughters. I wanted to take the secrets that I have learned over the years and condense them into a "just-the-facts" book that teenagers would enjoy. I have noticed that the majority of teenagers today are living their lives as if they are already grownup, creating schedules for themselves that don't allow much *peaceful* time. They seem to have forgotten that the purpose of being young is to *enjoy life* ... to enjoy the process of growing up. My attempt here is to give you some ideas that will help you create positive feelings and emotions—to create the life you want to live and be the person you want to be. I am confident that by the time you finish this book you will have been given the tools you need to know that *life is good*!

Judee Ausnow
Penn Valley, California
2007

CHAPTER ONE
MAKING CHOICES

My granddaughters have asked me over the years what I did before they were born. They say I must have been bored! I never realized what a joy it was to be a grandparent *and* what a learning experience it could be at the same time. I am blessed with two wonderful granddaughters who are finding their way in spite of the *drama* along the way. As they have grown into teenagers, the thing I have noticed more than anything else is the struggle teens have today with their peers. It seems to be the exception rather than the rule when teenagers are happy with their lives and feel confident and accepted, just being who they are.

The struggle seems to be the importance that is put on someone else's opinion of who you are. Don't allow someone else's opinion to determine how you feel about yourself. There is so much information and false images coming in from the media, the Internet, video games, and movies that put pressure on teens to look, act, and be something other than who they are. The answer is to empower yourselves with *who you are*. The fact that you have the power to make choices in your life is a huge plus. You can't always stop the judgments coming your way, but you can *always* stop the negative reaction *you* may have. You do *not* have to go around feeling bad—ever! Eleanor Roosevelt said "No one can make you feel inferior without your permission." That is an excellent statement to remember the next time you find yourself in the middle of conflict.

Have you ever noticed that you can't feel good and bad at the same time? Try a little experiment the next time you are feeling down and depressed: sing or laugh out loud. At first it may be hard to do because your *feelings* are not *feeling good*, but keep it up until you change the way you feel. Eventually you will feel good—you have no other choice. When you change the way you *think* about something, the way you *feel* will change. It is really that simple. We get in the habit of saying, "I'm just having a bad day." But there truly are no bad days; there is just our description of our day. At the end of every day, our feelings determine

1

how we describe our day, and we have the choice to *feel* any way we choose. Thoughts create our days *and* our lives and no one can tell us what to think, so *choose* good thoughts! It is difficult to believe sometimes, but the truth is that it's not what's happening around us that's making us unhappy, it is our *reaction* to it. So when we focus on feeling good we quit reacting and we create a good feeling in everything we do throughout the day. It's really not a complicated process. Pay attention to what makes you feel good and keep doing that.

And, be aware when your ego is running your life. Our egos always want to be right, but that often means a challenge with another person. When you're in the middle of conflict, ask yourself, What is the peaceful solution? And remind yourself that *you want to feel good*. Remember, staying peaceful is the goal, and it is also the most important way to keep your energy level strong.

We think that the world is full of matter, but it is really made up of energy. We consider our bodies to be made up of matter because they are solid and we can understand that. But quantum physics tells us that there is no matter in the universe. Everything—animate and inanimate, including us—is made up of energy. That energy creates the experiences we have in life. It creates both the good and the bad experiences by how we *choose* to think about our lives.

There is an experiment that was conducted in Japan with water. It is described in detail in the movie *What the Bleep Do We Know* (www.whatthebleep.com). The scientists tested water by a crystallization process that showed what the water's energy looked like. First they tested a sample of polluted water collected from the Fujiware Dam. Then they tested another sample of the same polluted water, only this second sample had been blessed by a Zen Buddhist monk. The energy pattern of the polluted water was dark and distressed, but the blessed water produced a beautiful crystal design that felt peaceful and good. Then they tested distilled water in bottles with words written on them. On one bottle they wrote words like *love* and *peace*. That water produced a beautiful pattern like the blessed water. On the other bottle they wrote words like *hate* and *killing*. That water, though "pure," produced an extremely distressed pattern like the polluted water. The water seemed to be reacting to the words written on the bottles. As they said in the movie, it makes you wonder, "If the energy from words can do that to water what do you think the energy from the negative words we have in our minds is doing to us?" Good question, don't you think?

Everything in our lives is energy. If we keep our energy strong we feel good; if we give our energy away we feel bad. Let's use money as an analogy—we can all relate to money! You start each day with $100 worth of life energy. Now, pay attention, because we're talking about *life energy* here—that's the stuff that keeps you alive. You get dressed and, while eating breakfast, you spill orange juice down the front of your clothes. You react in an angry way and there goes $20 worth of life energy. Then you get on the school bus and someone calls you a name or says something mean. You feel hurt and embarrassed, and there goes another $20 worth of life energy. When you get to school you realize you left your homework on the kitchen table and this is the final day to turn it in. You get upset and feel like you failed. There goes another $20 worth of life energy. And to top it off, your best friend says you're not invited to a special party. Wow—there goes $30. So, now you have only $10 worth of life energy left to get you through your entire day, and it's only nine o'clock in the morning. No wonder you feel as if life is difficult. There is no way we can feel good when our life energy is totally zapped. There is also no way to control every single thing that comes into our lives, so let's look at how you can keep your energy level high *while* getting through these challenges.

Go back to spilling the orange juice. How important is that in the big picture? Is it really worth $20 of your life energy? The truth is that the worst thing that would happen is that you are late for school and you need to prepare another set of clothes. It is not worth upsetting your entire life and zapping your energy—it's just a minor setback in this one particular day.

Let's take the issue of the mean kid on the school bus who called you a name. One of my granddaughters had that same experience when she was younger. I used to tell her to say to herself *that's not my truth* when someone called her a name or challenged her in some way. One day she actually said it out loud to a bully and his mouth fell open. He had no answer because it was not what he expected. He expected her to get upset and fight back, but instead she simply ended the issue by saying, "That's not my truth," and moving to another seat. Don't give anyone else power over you by making their opinion of you more important than your own opinion of yourself. Refuse to feel bad about yourself because someone else tells you to. Many times bullies are bullies because they don't know how to be nice. They feel badly about themselves and the only way they can feel better about themselves is to make someone else look worse in comparison. Sometimes, just refusing to react to their meanness can change the way they treat the next person who comes into their space. There's no fun in being mean if no one reacts to it.

Now, to the forgotten homework assignment. This is a challenge because this is the last day to turn it in. While teachers make rules to keep some kind of order in the classroom, they also may make an exception when asked in a kind way. The main thing to remember is to be honest about the reason that the assignment is not turned in. Telling the truth, regardless of what that is, always creates a better result than blaming something or someone else. I have experienced myself as a teenager that it is tempting to come up with some kind of excuse when something goes wrong, like, "The dog ate my homework!" It can be hard to take responsibility, but the end result is so much more empowering and satisfying when you can just be honest. So admit to forgetting your assignment at home and ask for the teacher's approval to bring it in the next day. Always ask yourself, *What is the worst thing that can happen from this experience?* In this case, you might have to do a make up assignment to catch up with your credits if the teacher will not make an exception. Regardless, it is not important enough to waste $20 worth of your *life energy* ... it is simply an inconvenience.

We all know that the real biggie in this day of misfortune is the party to which you've not been invited. If you are not invited to a special party, you need to ask yourself, *How special could it be if I'm not invited?* If you make an effort to be the best person you can be and treat others with kindness and respect, you will either be invited to the special parties, or the "special" parties are not really special after all. But whatever you do, do not allow someone else's choice to make any difference in how you feel about yourself.

There is nothing more important than the thoughts we choose when we think about ourselves. Those thoughts we hold inside us either make us feel good or bad about who we are. The *self talk* that we continually have each day either builds up our spirit or zaps our energy. Try a little test. Look in the mirror and say to yourself, *I love you.* If you are able to do this comfortably the first time, you are the exception. I know a lot of adults who have never in their entire lives been able to look into their own eyes and say those words. Think about it ... why would it be so hard to say *I love you* to yourself? Why would it be so hard to look yourself in the eye and feel good about who you are? It's all about programming. We are programmed from the time we are little children that loving ourselves is being conceited. Loving yourself has nothing to do with being conceited. Conceit has to do with who we are on the surface, especially when we strive to appear to be better than someone else. Loving yourself is about your spirit. It's about loving who you are on the inside. It's about being happy with who you are because happiness is an *inside job*. Happiness is what you bring to life, not something you get out of life.

So do this exercise every day and you will see a change take place. If you make a point to start each day looking into your own eyes and saying *I love you* to yourself, you will gain an abundance of self confidence and self love that will change your life. Try it. Laugh out loud if you have to, but commit to making this small change in your life *now*. If we can't love ourselves, why would we expect anyone else to love us? And, when we love ourselves, we are not only able to love others, others also love us back. It's a win-win situation that is filled with joy. Remember, we do not love because we *are loved*; we are loved because *we love*. Always choose love because it feels good. And, we're not talking about romantic love here. Romantic love can sometimes be shallow and fleeting. The kind of love we are talking about is genuine, respectful, caring and cooperative—the kind of love that comes from your spirit.

Making choices also relates to how we see the end result of an issue. If you want to create an experience and don't know how to do it, envision the result you want to have as if it has already been created in your life. Don't concentrate on why this choice can't happen—see it as if it has already materialized. Maybe you want to get an A on a test. Along with studying, *see* the A on the paper when you get it returned to you. *Feel* what it would feel like. How many times have you heard yourself say or heard your friends say things like, "I know I didn't do well on that test!" or, "I'm not good at math!"? And then, when the test comes back, sure enough, the grade is disappointing. If you don't believe that you are capable of receiving an A, it will never appear on your paper, regardless of how hard you study. It is like a Republican voting one way and Democrat voting the other—one vote cancels out the other. Your belief that it can't happen is enough to cancel out all the studying in the world. It costs you nothing to keep good, positive thoughts in your mind, choose to *think from the end*. Choose to create good energy with your thoughts.

There is a book called *Power vs. Force*, written by David Hawkins, M.D. Dr. Hawkins also believes that energy affects our lives. He describes a way of testing the energy in our bodies by something called *kinesiology,* or muscle testing. If you want to see how it works in *your* life, try this test. Stand erect, close your eyes, and take a few deep breaths. Then, with one hand, hold a piece of fruit (preferably organic) next to your heart. Hold your other arm out to your side, parallel to the floor, palm down, and elbow straight. Have someone push down on your wrist with two fingers. The idea is to push just hard enough to test the spring in your arm, not hard enough to cause the muscle to fatigue. You will be strong and the other person will be unable to make your arm go down. Now, put the fruit down and hold something that is not good for your body next to your heart—artificial sweetener or a CD with offensive words and music. Try the test again and your arm will go down easily. You can do this test with thoughts instead of things. When you think about something that makes you happy, your arm will be strong. When you think about something that makes you sad or angry, your arm will be weak. You can also test yourself. Make a "C" with the index finger and thumb of your left hand. While thinking of something you want to test, try to push your thumb and index finger together with the thumb and index finger of your right hand. If the choice is positive your fingers will be strong and you will feel the resistance. If your thought makes your fingers go together, making this choice will weaken your body.

The movies you choose to watch also have an enormous effect on your energy. If you are watching movies with a lot of violence in them, that energy is going to affect your feelings. Notice how you feel when you watch a comedy. When the movie ends you're happy and laughing. After you watch a movie that contains a lot of violence, you feel as if you have a lump in your stomach. Your feelings will not lie to you—pay attention to them. Before you buy a movie muscle test it to see if it has good energy.

By using these tools as guidelines you can determine what creates positive energy in your life and what creates negative energy—then you can make good choices so that your life works the way you want it to.

CHAPTER TWO
THOUGHTS ARE THINGS

There is no condition so severe that you cannot reverse it by choosing different thoughts. However, choosing different thoughts requires focus and practice. If you continue to focus as you have been, to think as you have been, and to believe as you have been, then nothing in your experience will change.
—Esther and Jerry Hicks, from their book *Ask and It Is Given: Learning to Manifest Your Desires*

Thoughts are things. Our life is created from our thoughts about it. Studies have shown that we have over 60,000 thoughts a day. The problem is that 90 percent of the thoughts we have today are the same thoughts we had yesterday and the day before and the day before and the day before that—no wonder we are tired all the time. Our minds are like computers, and the storage capacity is enormous. We keep thinking the same thoughts day after day. If those thoughts are positive, loving, and kind, our lives work great. If those thoughts are negative and judgmental, they create a feeling of depression and a what's-the-use kind of mentality. Many times the negative thoughts are about ourselves, and when we have that going on in our minds we have a prescription for depression: too heavy, too thin, not pretty enough, not smart enough, no one likes me ... you know the thoughts.

Remember one simple fact: *we get what we focus on.* So, why would we want to focus on the negative? Our thoughts are creating our lives. Let me repeat that: *OUR THOUGHTS ARE CREATING OUR LIVES!* When we really "get" that, we become really careful about what we think about all day long. In fact, I would suggest that each time you have a negative thought that doesn't feel good, stop and ask yourself, "Is this thought going to help me or hurt me?" If it's going to hurt you, refuse to think it—change it to a thought that feels good. Also, think about this simple question: "How would I feel if I didn't have this thought?" That question instantly creates a feeling of peace—it makes

7

you aware that it is simply the *thought* that feels bad. That is how powerful you are. *YOU* control your thoughts. Why would you want to continue to get more of what you *don't* want in your life? It is just not enough to say, "Why does this keep happening to me?" *Take responsibility!* "What goes in must come out" is not a saying that applies only to our bodies; it also applies to our minds. What we think about expands and creates more of the same. Why would you want to re-live the experiences over and over again that have made you sad in your life? Think about that. You are actually re-living the same experience each time you tell a friend your story. Make a decision right now to stop doing that to yourself.

There have been many accounts over the years of people who have been imprisoned (Nelson Mandela comes to mind) who have refused to hold on to negative thoughts. They have come out of devastating situations feeling better than they ever have in their lives. Nelson Mandela chose to remain at peace, even in the worst of circumstances. He said, "To make peace with an enemy, one must work with that enemy and that enemy becomes one's partner." He knew that if he let anger and hatred rule his life, he would become an angry, bitter man. The difference between him and the other prisoners was that he made a conscious effort to choose his thoughts. He was in prison for twenty-seven years, and after his release he became president of South Africa, improving the lives of millions of people. He is one of the greatest examples of people who have created their lives with their thoughts.

There are many other accounts of people who have been injured and unable to train for the sports they perform. Each day *in their minds* they have gone through a process of "seeing" themselves making the basket, getting a hole in one, or catching a long pass. They come back to the sport as confident and successful as they were before the injury. Their strength and success was manifested through their thoughts—simply with their thoughts. How powerful is that?

Almost everyday when my daughter was a sophomore in high school she would go through the same drama each morning. When her hair wouldn't come out the way she wanted it to, she would throw the curling iron on the floor. Needless to say, we went through a lot of curling irons. The interesting thing to me today is that I continued to buy them! Now I know that all I was doing by buying more curling irons was reinforcing the fact that her hair wouldn't be OK. Each day before she even started drying her hair, she had already made the decision *in her mind* what the outcome would be—her hair wouldn't cooperate, she'd throw the curling iron, and Mom would buy another one. Remember, what we think about expands. And where do we get the thoughts? From our experiences. Her experience with her hair was that it would not do what she wanted it to do. Then one day someone came up to her at school and said "your hair looks great". From that moment on she was able to get ready for school without the drama of her hair. Why is it that someone else can tell us something and we believe them, but we won't believe our own eyes? I say again, we get what we focus on. That is one of the most important lessons you will get out of this book.

Our habit tends to be to focus on what we don't want—that friend who said something mean, the test we failed, the extra weight on our body (our hair that won't do what we want it to do). Use your power to change your negative thoughts and watch your life change before your eyes. It IS that easy. We are the ones who make it difficult by thinking negative thoughts. No matter what is happening in your life—what's working and what's not working—you can figure out what thoughts you need to change.

There is another topic I'd like to touch on in this chapter. It's about *being in the moment.* This is a wonderful gift we can give ourselves. Be here now. Be present in your life. Live this day—not yesterday, not tomorrow—this day! The truth is that this is the only day we have. We are here today, so enjoy it. It is really impossible to live in the past or in the future. The decisions we make today are the ones that shape our lives and create joy or heartache—whichever we choose to allow. It is so exciting to have a choice each day to create our lives. The first thing I say as I am getting out of bed each morning is, "Thank You God for this day," and the next thing is, "I wonder what we can create today?" Saying these words reminds me that I am an *active participant* in life and not just going through the motions. What power to be able to create our lives with our thoughts!

Here's an example of how our thoughts affect us: Have you ever known someone who is accident prone? Hundreds of kids can go down the same stairs all day long but when the accident prone girl goes down she twists her ankle. Everyone else plays softball without getting hurt, but the accident prone guy gets hit by the ball. If you talk to these people you will see two things about them: One, they believe they are accident prone; and, two, they are not conscious of living in the moment. They are concerned about what is happening *to them* instead of being conscious of how *they* are *creating what is happening to them* with their thoughts.

Be present in everything you do. Be aware of your surroundings, pay attention to the step you are placing your foot on when you walk down the stairs, and be conscious of your posture. Be present instead of simply going through the motions. As you go out into your world *see* it the way you want it to be. See the A on the test, see the smile on your face, see yourself getting to school and back safely, see yourself eating good food to nourish your body, see your friends having a great day. Make it a habit to want for others what you want for yourself. It is much easier to go through life with friends who are living lives filled with happy experiences than with friends who are always in the middle of a drama, so want for others what you want for yourself. Make each day an experiment. See if it makes a difference to choose good thoughts of perfect health, joy, and peace in your life … I am betting it will.

CHAPTER THREE
THE SECRET TO HEALTHY WEIGHT

This life is a blessing. Take care of it and take care of yourself. The body that carries you from place to place is the garage for your soul. After all, we are spiritual beings having a human experience, not the other way around. Honor your body, feed it good thoughts, and watch your life turn around. And while you are at it, feed your body good, nourishing food. There is an epidemic today of overweight teenagers. Have you ever wondered why? I have come to believe that the primary reason so many of us have trouble controlling our weight is *continued negative thoughts* involving our weight: the guilt each time we take a bite of food, the constant worry that food equals fat. Those thoughts create increased fat on our bodies because what we think about manifests; in this case, our fat expands! If we are continually thinking that we are overweight, we continue to do the things that created the excess weight in the first place. We fall into the feeling of "what's the use," and then we use food to comfort ourselves. Does this sound familiar? You get up in the morning and look in the mirror. You vow to never eat again until you lose weight. You refuse to eat all day, and then when you are starved you eat everything in sight. That's just the opposite of what your body really needs. *Our bodies need nourishment* and when they don't get it, they go into the I'm-being-starved mode and start storing fat for survival. If you are overweight, eat more often not less often. Start eating six *small* meals a day, and always start with a good nourishing breakfast like eggs and oatmeal—not sugary cereals. Your body needs breakfast to start your metabolism working. Never let your metabolism go into fat-saving mode. When you are eating six small, good-for-you meals a day you are never so hungry that you will binge. There are so many good choices out there. Don't make good eating into a "diet." Choose to eat good foods like fruit, chicken, fish, vegetables and grains. Raw almonds are one of the best nourishing foods you can eat—they taste great and you can carry some in your pocket. A good rule of thumb is to eat fresh food, not packaged food, and eliminate sugar as much as possible. I've found it amazing how much good food you can wrap up into a "wrap." Combine fish or chicken, veggies, lettuce, and even some fruit. The flavors are great together. Grab an apple or a handful of raw almonds when you need a lift. Keep your backpack or purse filled with good snacks.

Make it a habit to eat breakfast as early as you possibly can, and lunch between 12-1:30 PM. Eat the majority of the food you consume each day at breakfast and lunch because that is the time your metabolism is at its peak, and your body burns the most calories. This practice will create a balanced rhythm in your eating pattern and make it easier to eat a smaller dinner, without feeling deprived. If you are hungry in the afternoon, eat a good snack a couple of hours before dinner to help raise your metabolism. Also, give your body a break and don't eat after 7:00 PM (or at least three hours before bedtime) so your digestive tract can do its job to process the foods you've taken in during the day. This practice will allow the food to digest *before* you go to bed. That is one of the main reasons people are overweight. When they eat late—including desert—and then go to bed, the food just turns to excess fat.

In his CD series *Mind/Body Nutrition*, nationally recognized teacher, speaker, and nutrition consultant, Marc David, tells about a study that was conducted with a group of people eating a 2000 calorie diet. They were instructed to eat the entire 2000 calories at just one meal—breakfast, lunch or dinner. The same people were tested over the course of the study to determine what time of day their bodies burned the most calories. When they ate the meal at breakfast they either lost weight or maintained their weight. When they ate the meal at lunch they all lost weight. But when they ate the meal at dinner they all gained weight. He says, "*When* you eat is as important as *what* you eat." So, burn those calories early in the day when your metabolism is up and running.

Practice eating simple. Eliminate the extra sauces on foods, and if you can't live without some french fries once in a while, eat only a few and don't dunk them in ranch dressing. Drink water instead of soft drinks … just making this one change will do wonders for your health and your weight. Don't buy (or ask your parents for) the foods that keep you overweight, so you are not tempted to eat them. Take a course on nutrition or get a good book that will walk you through the steps to change the way you eat for life. I just finished a book by Tosca Reno called *The Eat-Clean Diet*. Don't let the title fool you—it's really *not* a "diet" book. She talks about a lot of the things I have mentioned in this chapter—in detail—and, she has lost 70 pounds using the ideas she offers in her book. Eating clean is a way of life that teaches you *how* to eat. The book explains why certain foods are needed by our bodies, and why diets don't work. It's easy to read, and filled with wonderful ideas to keep your metabolism revved up. As Tosca says, "The average teen now gets a whooping one-fifth of his or her daily calories from sugar and it is not even a food group!" That's something to think about. If you are eating a 2000 calorie diet, just eliminating the sugar cuts 400 calories.

Trust yourself for once—you can make changes in your weight and health … and do it for you. For the next two weeks *be present* when you eat, pay attention to everything that goes into your mouth, and allow only the foods that will nourish your body. Try the "muscle test" to see how your body responds to the food you've chosen. Create a habit to change your eating habits. It is simply the habit you are *currently* in that has created the weight, and you have the power to change it! When you truly realize you are what you eat, you become really careful about what you put in your mouth. The truth is, after you eat, you're full regardless of what you've eaten, so choose foods that nourish your body and create good health.

See yourself the way you want to look and feel. This is truly the most important thing you can do to lose weight and create the body you want to have. Look in the mirror and *see* the person you choose to be. William James, the father of modern psychology, put it this way: "There is a law in psychology that if you form a picture in your mind of what you would like to be, and you keep and you hold that picture there long enough, you will soon become exactly as you have been thinking." See yourself in a healthy, fit body. See yourself buying the clothes that make your heart smile. See yourself playing the sports you have always wanted to play—and feeling great. When we change our thoughts to healthy thoughts and see our bodies the way we want them to be, we literally change the way we choose the food we eat. We become more aware of this body that God gave us and we start choosing food that nourishes our bodies … *and* we start to lose weight. We even start to *want* to do things that help the process—like walking or exercising. Sign up for a dance class or get a dance video that you can use at home. Most of you have probably seen *Dancing with the Stars* on TV. A good workout at a dance class can burn as much as 700 calories—and look at the fun you'll have.

Another important part of this process of changing your thoughts is to be willing to *feel your feelings*—to recognize them for what they are. Sometimes it's difficult to pin down our feelings because they come at us so fast and they get mixed up together. If you need help recognizing your feelings, take a pad of paper and write yourself a letter about all the feelings you have had from the time the extra weight started to show up on your body. Remember each time you have felt bad about yourself because of the weight and write that down. It's easier to pretend the problem doesn't exist and continue to do things the same way, but to create change you need to eliminate the *feelings* that keep you trapped in the overweight body. So write them down, forgive yourself for spending so much time on them, and let them go for good. This is a good time to use the question in chapter two: "How would I feel if I didn't have this thought"? After you have written the letter, read it over as many times as you need to until you *feel* that you can release these feelings and *create a new you.* Then release the feelings for good by having a little ceremony: burn the letter in the fireplace or tear it up into little pieces. *Then get moving and make a commitment to yourself to have the healthiest body you can create.*

I was not born with the body of a super model, but when I was a teenager we walked everywhere, starting with two miles to school. I know what you're thinking … what, no snow? I grew up in southern California, so I wasn't trudging through a foot of snow on my way to school like some of your grandparents did, but I realize that walking two miles to and from school kept my friends and I from experiencing the weight problems many teens have today. In addition, we didn't have fast food restaurants on every corner. Fast food to us meant getting a pan out of the cabinet and cooking something as fast as we could—or eating a piece of fruit. Yes, we had candy bars and sweets, but we were walking off those extra calories. We also had "real" gym classes and were required to participate in some form of exercise each day.

Today's teens get a ride to and from school, plop down in front of the TV when they get home, and every commercial is about food—mostly fat-building foods. You gain weight, go on crazy diets, and get disappointed when you don't lose weight. Being on a "diet" makes us feel deprived. We force ourselves to eat things we don't even like until we loose a few pounds, and then, when we reach our goal, we reward ourselves with the food we missed—putting the weight back on and feeling like failures once more. Feeling like a failure is actually what keeps the weight on, because when you feel badly enough about yourself you just give up.

How often do you see a commercial about home cooked good-for-you meals on television? Why do you think the majority of the commercials you do see are selling hamburgers and french fries ... because they are good for your health or because the fast food industry is a multi-billion dollar business? Don't you think it's time for you to *take your power back* and quit supporting fast food restaurants that do not have *your health* as their primary concern? Make your health your number one priority and make these restaurants earn your business by selling healthy food.

The answer is to see yourself as you want to be, choose good food and get moving. When you go to the mall, make a commitment to walk the entire circle at least twice, and then reward yourself with shopping. Get a friend to walk with you several times a week instead of spending lots of time in front of the TV or computer after school. If the area you live in is unsafe to walk or doesn't have a walking path, walk around school throughout the day, even if it's only ten minutes at a time. Every little bit helps, not only your weight but your health. All you have to do is see yourself as you want to be, make a commitment to yourself—*nobody else*—to be as healthy as you can be and keep that commitment until you create a habit. You created a habit that added the weight, so create a new habit that will change your life.

When we start treating our bodies as the greatest gift we have been given, and honor them for the fantastic job they do for us each day, we become very careful about what goes into them. We all know people who have lots of material stuff, great bodies, and lots of money, but don't have good health. Good health is not the way our bodies look on the outside; good health is the way our bodies *are* on the inside, and that is determined by what goes into them—period. Many of you are very protective of your cars. You would never put something in the gas tank that would hurt the engine—so don't do it to your body. You are what you eat!

CHAPTER FOUR
CHOOSING FORGIVENESS

Forgiveness is probably the most misunderstood gift we can give to ourselves. Most people have a difficult time with forgiveness—they often think the "other person" doesn't deserve to be forgiven. They don't understand that forgiveness is *not* for the other person, it is for them. When we choose to hold on to judgments, hurts, and resentments we are only hurting ourselves. Most of the time the other person isn't even aware that we are causing ourselves pain over the situation. Most of the time, for the other person, *it is over.* The other person continues with life while we drag ourselves around with *baggage* weighing us down.

Visualize this … you have a suitcase, and each time you refuse to forgive someone—friends, family, parents, teachers, even strangers—you put the *baggage* of that inability to forgive into that suitcase. Now, you are responsible for this suitcase so you need to carry it with you at all times—everywhere. Each time you refuse to forgive, that suitcase gets heavier and heavier. If you are really good at non-forgiveness, you may find yourself shopping for a five-piece set of luggage! Very quickly this can become a full time burden, leaving no time for joy in your life. Why would you want to do this to yourself?

Look in the mirror and think about a person you refuse to forgive. Your facial features literally change before your eyes. Notice how unattractive you become. That is what hate does to us—not only on the outside but on the inside as well. Eventually on the inside it creates illness. Remember, everything is energy. When we short circuit our energy with feelings of hatred we create illnesses. If you have a friend who is always sick, ask yourself if there are people or circumstances in her life that she is unwilling to forgive—things that she holds onto and talks about every day, causing her to re-live them over and over again. Do your friend a favor and refuse to hear her story the next time she wants to tell it to you. Ask her with kindness why she would want to re-live that experience one more time in her life. Suggest that she *let it go* for her sake, and make her aware how much her personality changes when she is in the middle of the pain that it causes her. That would truly be *being her friend*. (And, although our example here is a "her," this applies to guys, too.)

When my granddaughters were little girls, I gave them each a beautiful book called *The Little Soul and the Sun*, written by Neale Donald Walsh. It is a children's book about a little boy angel who wants God to send him to earth so he can learn to forgive. The pictures in the book show all of the little boy and girl angels in heaven with big smiles on their faces, enjoying the peace and love that they feel there. God says to the little boy angel that the only way he can learn forgiveness is if one of the other little angels would be willing to go to earth with him to give him a reason to forgive. He looks around and tells God he can't ask anyone to go to earth and leave this beautiful place … it is so peaceful here. At that moment a little girl angel comes forward and tells him she will go to earth with him so he can learn to forgive. All she asks of him is that when he is in the middle of the hurt and pain that she will need to cause him in order for him to learn to forgive … to please remember *Who She Truly Is*."

I didn't understand the real meaning of that book until years later. You see, it's not what happens to us, it's our *reaction to what happens to us* that really matters. The test is whether we are able to forgive. And remember that every person started out on this earth as a perfect little boy or girl "angel" who just got off track. There will always be people in our lives whom we will need to forgive until we learn to choose forgiveness in every situation—then we don't need that lesson any longer. When challenges appear in our lives they are simply opportunities to choose love instead of resentment and hatred. *The enemy is not the people we choose to hate, the enemy is hatred itself*. The only way to change the hatred is to release the feelings we have for certain people—and it doesn't really matter who those people are. You see, they are doing what they are doing so we can learn to forgive.

There's another side of forgiveness that is extremely important—it's about forgiving *ourselves*. We can be our own worst enemy. It is impossible to live on this earth with six billion people and not be given opportunities to feel ashamed, embarrassed, unworthy, or like we have failed in some way. Unless we stay in a room by ourselves for our entire lives, we will be given many opportunities to feel badly about ourselves. That's just the way life works.

Now, if you have read the first two chapters of this book, you have the tools to understand that you *never* have to feel ashamed, embarrassed, unworthy, or like you have failed—*never*. You create your life with your thoughts, so when you are given an opportunity—and you will be—to feel any of these emotions, ask yourself these questions: By feeling ashamed, embarrassed, unworthy, or like a failure, will I change the situation that caused it? Will I feel good about myself? The answer to both is NO! Hindsight has never changed a situation that has already occurred, and feeling bad about *you* only makes the situation worse and creates more negativity. These opportunities come into our lives not to beat us down and make us feel bad, but to give us the opportunity to forgive ourselves.

We would never learn to forgive ourselves—we would never even know what forgiving ourselves meant—if we were not given a reason to do it. If our actions have hurt another, it is an opportunity to take responsibility and apologize, asking for their forgiveness. There is always good in everything that happens to us, even if you can't see it in the moment. Everything has its opposite; good/bad, hot/cold, happy/sad, even hatred/forgiveness. We would not even recognize a happy moment if there were never a sad one to compare it to. It is all good—we just get to choose how we *allow* it to affect our lives. The better we get at forgiveness, the less we need to experience it in our lives … reasons truly stop showing up. Learn to be your own best friend and give yourself the same benefit of the doubt that you are willing to give to your friends. Give yourself the understanding that you're doing the best you can and God isn't finished with you yet. Do the best you are capable of in life, be the best person you can be, and when these moments happen, choose to love and forgive yourself. You get what you focus on and, if your focus is on what you have done that you are not happy with, you will be given more of the same, so stop it right now. Refuse to do that to yourself any longer. Be your own best friend and show yourself the same love and respect that you would show any best friend. We all make mistakes. I believe the test is to strive to be better than we used to be. We should never make life a competition with anyone else. After all, it really isn't between you and others anyway; it is always between you and God.

I recently read a book, that I would like to recommend, called *Left to Tell* written by Immaculee Ilibagiza. This book enabled me to totally understand the power of forgiveness. Immaculee is a survivor of the 1994 Rwandan Holocaust in which one million people were brutally killed. She not only survived, she was able to forgive the people—some she had known her entire life—who were responsible for killing her mother, father, and two brothers. She hid in a three-foot-by-four-foot bathroom with seven other women for ninety-one days and her weight dropped to sixty-five pounds—and she is 5' 9" tall. It is an incredible book about faith, strength, courage, and the powerful gift of forgiveness. For me, learning about other people's struggles quickly puts my little complaints into perspective and I am able to appreciate more fully the life I live.

CHAPTER FIVE
CREATING GOOD RELATIONSHIPS

Relationships are the real test of living on this earth, and they *really* exist *only* in your mind. If you don't believe that statement, think about someone you are in a relationship with—someone who is not in the room as you are reading this. At this moment you are thinking about this person with your mind. Your relationship is determined by what you are thinking *in this moment*. Let's use your parents as an example. If you have experienced a loving and kind relationship with them for most of your life, your thoughts of them will most likely be loving and kind. If you consider your parents to be hard on you and always wanting more from you than you are capable of giving, your relationship with them, *in your mind*, may be painful and unhappy.

Each time you feel resentful toward someone, ask yourself how you are *seeing* that person in your mind. Surround yourself with thoughts of what you want to create in your relationship and remember the times the relationship has been good. If your feelings are always resentful, each time you are around this person your attitude will be resentful—and if it is not obvious on the outside, it is always obvious on the inside. Our bodies respond to our feelings. If we walk into a room and see someone we've decided we don't like, our bodies stiffen up and the look on our face changes whether we are conscious of it or not. I am using the word *decided* for a good reason, because we *decide* how we will treat someone else by feelings we have gained from past experiences we may have had with this person. If we *create* the relationship in our minds, we can also *change* the relationship in our minds. Choose to *see* the relationship as you would like it to be. See the two of you talking and having a wonderful conversation that feels good. Take a few deep breaths when you are in these situations and notice the difference in your energy and feelings. *Practice* having the experience you want with this person as if it is already happening—and watch it appear.

It seems that there is not a lot of forgiving going on today, but there is a lot of holding on to judgments and opinions about other people. Teens seem to love to use cell phones, text messaging, and IM to tell everyone who will listen how much they hate certain people. The focus seems to be to get everyone else they know to hate the same people, too, because that is the only way they can really justify their behavior—otherwise *they* look like a bully. Much of the time their reasoning is based on a single instance when someone made a mistake or caused hurt in some way. Opinions are determined at that moment and every time the same people are together that memory remains, creating judgment in everything else that happens. Many times it wouldn't matter how much the other person is trying to be kind because the *opinion* has already been made. Our judgments usually surface because we are offended by someone else's choice—we are disappointed that they don't see things our way. You probably know people who choose to be offended by almost everything—people who always have an opinion about everything and use every chance to convince you they are right. The greatest gift you can give someone like this is to *see* them, *in your mind*, making choices to be more loving toward others and being able to give the benefit of the doubt. See them being kind to themselves and others. "Imagination is everything, it is the preview of life's coming attractions."—Albert Einstein. We can all change the way we treat others at any moment we choose. All we need to do is make an intention to change the way we think. What we intend in our minds we will create in our lives.

I'd like to use the following story as an example to show how much our judgment determines our relationships. I was introduced to a woman many years ago, and my first impression was that she didn't look or act as I thought she should. She didn't seem to care about how she dressed or what she looked like. Her attitude seemed to me to be one of not caring about others and only being concerned about herself. Her tone of voice lacked enthusiasm and my short conversation with her zapped my energy. Needless to say, I didn't spend much time trying to get to know her. Then one day we had the opportunity to sit down and talk to each other. I was amazed to learn how talented, educated, and giving this person really was. After spending a few minutes talking to her I realized my previous judgment was just my ego sizing her up to my expectations of what I thought she should be. The exterior appearance I had been judging was nothing like the warm, friendly person I found her to be inside. It turned out that she not only provided financial support for a family member who had a long-term illness, she also served as primary caregiver. This created a lack of money for her to dress as she would have liked to. She got very little sleep every night, and had very little energy to spend trying to get people to like her. Her weariness also affected her tone of voice. What was amazing to me is after we had this conversation and formed a friendship, her voice sounded totally different to me. I told other people how nice this person was, and as a result they began to treat her differently. Eventually my new friend's whole attitude *seemed* to change. I must admit, I have never really known whether her attitude really changed or, if by *changing the way I saw her,* I got to see her attitude as it *really* was.

We have many opportunities each day to see others as they truly are and not as we expect them to be. Make it your intention to be nonjudgmental for a day. Give up your need to judge others and pay attention to what they have to say. You will be amazed how much you can learn about someone by just asking them a few questions and then truly listening to their response. We easily say to our friends, "How are you?" Unless the person is a chronic complainer the answer is usually, "Fine." Try asking your friends questions that will enable you to really get to know them like, "What makes your heart smile?" or "What is the best thing that has ever happened to you?" Then really *listen* to their responses. Be the kind of person you would want to be friends with. Get to know your friends instead of just going through the motions. And get to know the so called "strangers" in your school. Remember, strangers are simply people we haven't made friends with yet ... they could turn out to be your best friends.

CHAPTER SIX
THE FAMILY

There are no mistakes. When God created families he knew what he was doing. Families can be the greatest challenges we have in life. They can also be the source of the greatest lessons we will ever learn. It is in the family environment that we as little children are intended to get our start in life—a place where we can feel loved, cared for, and accepted—a place where we can feel safe. Each person in a family is there for a reason: to round out the personalities needed to make the family work, through all the challenges the family will face. Look at your own family. Look at its strengths and weaknesses. It would be easy to live in a family if no one ever rocked the boat, if everyone just went through life in the middle of the road with no ups or downs. But that's not the purpose of family. Family members are intended to love each other unconditionally regardless of the challenges they go through. God created families so we would choose love during the moments when it might be easier to choose hate and walk away. God gave us families to hold us accountable—hold us to that unconditional love that is so easy to talk about, but difficult at times to give. God gave us families to teach us to walk the walk not just talk the talk.

Take a moment to remember your life five years ago. If it was a peaceful time for you, the memory will be pleasant. If it wasn't peaceful, the memory may not feel good. The truth is that for everyone reading this, whatever happened in the last five years has brought you to today—to the lessons you have learned, the gifts you have been given, to the strength you have developed from each experience. We would not be who we are today without the experiences we have had. The only way to grow as a person in this world is to be the best person you can be *through the challenges*. The only way to grow as a family is to stay strong—even in the worst of circumstances—and to be there for each other.

I feel I need a disclaimer here because statistics show that 85 percent of families today are challenged by one serious situation or another. There are families with single parents (of which I am one and consider my greatest accomplishment in life). There are families in which physical or verbal abuse happens. And there are families struggling with alcoholism and drug abuse. I am not suggesting that you allow yourself to be abused in the name of family. I am hoping that the previous chapters have given you tools to give you the strength to make positive choices. If your family situation is physically abusive please remove yourself from the situation and get the help you need as quickly as possible. Talk to your school counselor or teacher for organizations in your area. There was a program on Lifetime Television about an organization called Childhelp that was founded in 1959 by two women: Sara O'Meara and Yvonne Fedderson. Their website is www.childhelp.org and their child abuse hotline is 1-800-4-A-CHILD. You are not even required to give your name if you don't choose to.

Sometimes in today's society, teens treat their siblings with much less respect than they do their friends. It is important to remember that friends may come and go, but your family is there when you need them. If we treated our friends the way we sometimes treat our family, we would be very lonely people because friends don't put up with disrespectful treatment for very long. Friends walk away if we treat them badly enough, often enough. Our families are the people we live with day in and day out. If you think about it, in most cases we do pretty well because any time there are more than one person in a room there is an opportunity for conflict. The only way to live peacefully in a home with other people is to treat them as you want to be treated yourself. When you have problems with family members, instead of reacting and yelling, take a moment and think about what you want to say and how you want to say it. Think about how you want family members to talk to you—practice the Golden Rule ... it's *golden* for a reason. Remember, once an unkind word is spoken it's almost impossible to take it back— the other person has already *felt* the feelings of hurt and unworthiness. Instead of saying things you may be sorry for later, make a list of all the things about the person that you love and respect. You will be surprised how many you can think of. After you have completed this process, give the list to the other person and watch his or her face light up. It will do more good than all the apologies in the world. Everyone wants to be acknowledged—especially family members—and your willingness to take the time to write down the positive will speak volumes.

In his CD series, *Inspiration*, Dr. Wayne W. Dyer tells about the Bamemba tribe who live in the northern part of South Africa. They practice an amazing ritual when someone in their tribe is not getting along with the others. They stop everything, put them in the center of a circle and everyone in the village takes turns telling them all the *good things* they remember about them—from the time they were born. They do this for days until everyone has had a chance to share these wonderful thoughts. Because of this process, the occasion for this to happen is about one person every five years. These fortunate people are given the opportunity to *remember* who they truly are.

When people do things to us that we don't like, we have the tendency to tell them how bad they are and how terrible they made *us* feel. No wonder people don't change their behavior and just want to get away from us as quickly as possible—they are feeling unworthy. When people in our families are having problems, it is our job to *love them through it,* not criticize them. Always put yourself in their shoes and ask yourself how you would feel in the same circumstances. Be willing to see *who they truly are* and not who they are projecting themselves to be in this single moment. The great twentieth-century teacher Abraham Maslow put it this way: "What is necessary to change a person is to change his awareness of himself." Be willing to help others see their magnificence.

A lot of damage is done to our self confidence by well-meaning family members. It's easy to think we know how other people feel and what is best for them. Most of the time there is little consideration for other people's feelings when we are trying to get them to believe what *we* think is right for them. We forget that the only way we have to relate is through our own experiences. The truth is that we *all* have our own experiences, and what we get out of them—good or bad—is as individual as we are. What is right for one person may not be right for another. The greatest gift we can give each other, as a family, is to allow all members to be the individuals that they showed up here to be—and bless them in the process. Unconditional love enables all family members to grow in their own way and be the people that make *their* hearts smile. We all have wonderful qualities and talents just waiting to be revealed, so be the person you were meant to be and, as Mark Twain said, "Work like you don't need the money. Love like you've never been hurt. Dance like no one is watching!" That is one of my most favorite sayings in the world—I even have it printed on my laundry room cabinet doors. It is a great reminder to me that my life is happening *now* and to enjoy everyday.

CHAPTER SEVEN
OUR CHARACTER

There is a major difference between our reputation and our character. It seems most people are concerned about their reputations—*what other people think of them.* Your reputation is simply someone else's opinion of who you are and not who you truly are at all. If you line up ten people and ask them what they think of you, you could easily get ten different answers. If you ask your best friend, the answer would usually be quite positive. If you ask a teacher, the answer could be determined by your grades or your behavior in class. If you ask acquaintances who really don't know you very well, the answers might be determined by what other people have said to them about you. Most of the time your concern about your reputation is that you want to feel like you belong—in school or with your group of friends. The problem is that always trying to *fit in* doesn't allow you to be yourself—or even allow you to know *who* you truly are. You're so busy trying to be what everyone else wants you to be that the star within never gets a chance to shine!

Your character, on the other hand, is who you truly are. It is what tells other people what you believe in, what is important to you, and what kind of person you really are. Your character is determined by how you live your life. If you choose to be loving, kind, and sincere about how you respond to others, your character is like a shinning star. It is your character that determines whether you choose to go along with the crowd even though you feel something is wrong, or stand up for what you believe in. When you choose what you know is right, your character is reminding you that you have to live with the decisions you make and that you must make the ones that allow your life to work in wonderful ways. When we are not true to our character we end up feeling bad about ourselves—we feel unworthy. Theodore Roosevelt said, "I care not what others think of what I do, but I care very much about what I think of what I do. That is character!"

Teenagers often find themselves in positions where they need to rely on their character. When you are put in situations where going along with the crowd can be dangerous to your health—when drugs or alcohol are involved, for example—it is very important to *know who you are* and not be willing to compromise *who you are* for anyone. Even at the risk of popularity, be true to yourself. *Pay attention to your feelings.* If it doesn't feel good in your heart, if you have any doubts that come up at all about the outcome, say *NO*. If you're a girl and your boyfriend is pressuring you to have sex, don't fall for it. You will know in your heart when that time is right for you. And with consequences like disease and pregnancy (which most often results in the inability to get an education) it is important to make those kinds of decisions carefully and not in the heat of the moment. Always remember that you have nothing to prove, and any boy worth having in your life will not pressure you into doing something you don't want to do, just to prove that you love him. While marrying your high school sweetheart sounds romantic, it doesn't happen very often. And, sometimes when it does, it is *because* of pregnancy and the marriage doesn't last. Do not discredit yourself to please a boyfriend … it is just not necessary. This is *your life* we are talking about. Don't make rash decisions that can take away your future and your joy.

There have been many shows on Lifetime Television about this subject. These are real-life stories about *real-life kids* who have made decisions they have later regretted. There are stories about fourteen and fifteen-year-old girls who are willing to have sex just because boys expect it—because everyone else is doing it. What are they thinking? Ask yourselves what kind of reputation you will get from those actions and what kind of damage that will do to your character. Going along with the crowd, whether it relates to sex, drugs, alcohol or even smoking is not very smart. These are decisions that can ruin your life … these are decisions that can kill you. When you finally understand that each and every one of you is a child of God, you will begin to treasure your life and your character and you won't want to do anything to discredit yourself. You are the most important possession you have, so treat *yourself* with kindness and respect.

When you are true to yourself, love yourself, and feel good about who you are, everything else falls into place. You realize that you do not need to keep searching for a boyfriend or girlfriend to feel that you are important and complete. You start to enjoy your own company and seldom find yourself getting bored—which is the main reason you think you need another person in order to feel good in the first place. When you are content with your own company and enjoy spending quiet time alone, you get to know who you truly are instead of putting all your attention on someone else. You give up the full-time job of needing to know what another person is doing all the time and you also release the need to be jealous. When you learn to love yourself, you realize that if a boyfriend or girlfriend decides to date someone else, he or she was never worthy of you in the first place. There is no greater power than knowing how valuable you are as a human being. And when you know that, you will attract a boyfriend or girlfriend who knows that too. Then when the right relationship comes along, it is made up of two confident and emotionally balanced people who add to each other's lives and are not afraid to be who they truly are. You will have a relationship between two people who are "relating" to each other from the happiness and perfection they have within themselves instead of from their egos—what a concept!

So many teens today are programmed to be constantly on the go that when things are quiet they feel like something is wrong. Start paying attention to how many hours you spend on your cell phone, text messaging or IM. I think you will be surprised how much of your time is consumed in these activities. Also, pay attention to how many of those messages and phone calls are negative conversations—usually gossiping about someone else. Well, I've got good news and bad news. The bad news is—negative talk is hazardous to your character. The good news is—you can change to a positive response at any moment you choose. When someone is talking about someone else in a negative way, choose to be the one to stick up for the underdog. We have all been the one being talked about at some time in our lives. There are always two sides to every story, and most of the time the negative side is exaggerated. At the very least, don't jeopardize your character just to hear yourself talk … change the subject.

CHAPTER EIGHT
INTENTION AND INSPIRATION

Two of the most powerful books I have read by Dr. Wayne W. Dyer are *The Power of Intention* and *Inspiration: Your Ultimate Calling*. I realize that when I am aware of these two processes in my own life, and use them for my highest good, my life works so much easier. Let me explain what I mean.

When we want something to happen or to change in our lives, most of us *wish* for it and try to *force* it to happen. There is a much easier and more peaceful way to create good in our lives—by placing an *intention* and holding onto that thought as if it already existed. Dr. Dyer explains this process as "thinking from the end."

Intention is *similar* to the law of attraction—what you focus on you create in your life. The difference is intention is putting out to the universe those thoughts you want to create *intentionally*. Then, the law of attraction takes those thoughts and produces the results in your life. Learn to pay attention to the feelings within you that are urging you to do something you may never have done before. Feelings that keep surfacing like you need to make a phone call, take a certain class or participate in some new activity. These are usually intuitive feelings that are urging you to make positive changes in your life. To step outside the box and move beyond the limits you have created for yourself.

Make a decision right now to place your intention and follow through with that intention on anything you want to change in your life. If you are struggling in school, make an intention to allow more time to study each day. Most of you are in school a minimum of thirty-five hours a week, so why waste that time? Get the very most you can out of the process. You are putting the time in whether you get good grades or not, so go for the good grades. You will be surprised what a little *quality* study time will do for you—and be sure to be *conscious* of the *intention* to bring your grades up. Change your thinking from "have to" to "choose to" when you think about your school work. Develop an intention to "choose" to be a good student and watch the incredible change take place before your very eyes. Every time you think about what kind of a student you are and what assignment is coming due, see yourself getting an A ... even if right now it seems silly. It works, so what do you have to lose?

Actually, intention is how all of this information became a book. I created a mock cover and hung copies of it in several places around my house—for me my bathroom mirror works great. Every time I read the words I visualized this book displayed on tables in bookstores and in the hands of teens around the world. I saw it making a difference in your lives. So, if you are reading this right now, can you believe the power of intention works? I can! Take the steps to make the power of intention work in your life and while you are at it, add a little inspiration.

This quote by the ancient Indian philosopher Patanjali says it all: "When you are inspired ... dormant forces become alive, and you discover yourself to be a greater person by far than you ever dreamed yourself to be."

Dr. Dyer describes inspiration as "being in-Spirit." He says, "Being inspired is an experience of joy: we feel completely connected to our Source and totally on purpose...."

There are many religions and many names for God. Regardless of our choice of religion, the thing to remember is that underneath it all we are spiritual beings having a human experience. What that means is that each of us is not simply a physical body that carries us around, each of us is *what is inside.* There is a source inside of us that beats our hearts and puts breath into our bodies—regardless of what we call it. *This source is not just in some of us—it is in every one of us.* We feel this presence the strongest when we feel passionate about something. Dr. Dyer says, "Just the fact that we're interested and excited about doing something is all the evidence we need—this is inspiration right in front of us, begging us to pay attention to the feeling." Let yourself feel this presence within you, pay attention to these feelings, and start living a life of inspiration.

Be the greatest person you can be. Live an inspired life, paying attention to your behaviors and attitudes, and thinking positive, inspired thoughts. You will know if you are living an inspired life if you are creating good results—if you're feeling good about who you are and what you do each day. You'll also start attracting other people who are living from inspiration. You'll find that life gets much more peaceful because you are sending peaceful vibrations out into the world and attracting them back to you.

Inspiration is also created by our feelings. It is not only what you *think* about, it is what you *feel* that is so important. Thoughts and *feelings* create your life, moment by moment. If something is not working for you right now, recognize your feelings about what is going on in your life. You can do this with everything in your life: health, school, family, or relationships. There are only two types of feelings: good feelings and bad feelings. Joy, peace, and love are good feelings. Hate, frustration, and jealousy are bad feelings. By creating feelings that make you feel good, you will be living from a place of inspiration. Living an inspired life just *feels good*. You start each day being happy to be alive and looking forward to your day. You have the choice to make your day as good as it gets—by your thoughts and inspiration.

Also, use *visualization* each day as you awake and *see* the day you would like to have. There is scientific proof that we can use the process of visualization to create reality in our lives. Dr. Dennis Waitley took the visualization process that had been developed for the Apollo program and used it in the Olympic training program during the 1980s and 1990s with great success. The athletes were hooked up to biofeedback machines during the performance of their sport, and again while they were just thinking about performing their sport. The biofeedback levels were the same whether they were performing physically or just visualizing the performance in their minds. The same muscles were activated in each instance because thoughts drive the body. There is a great DVD called *The Secret* (www.thesecret.tv) that explains this process and the law of attraction, which I will talk about in the next chapter.

I remember a story Tony Robbins, who is a well-known motivational speaker, told about his childhood. When he was eight years old he attended a third-grade class where the students were already learning division in math. Division was new to Tony and he had a hard time with it. His teacher considered him a poor student—not very smart—and said so quite often. He felt bad about himself and felt like a failure. Then his family moved to another town, and Tony was sent to a new school. His new class had not started division yet so, when they did, he already knew more than the rest of the class. Since he was always the first one finished with his math tests, his new teacher kept saying how smart he was. She gave him extra assignments and asked him to help her with projects in the class. He began to feel good about himself (inspired) and decided that he was smart after all. This experience helped him to become the successful person he is today. The moral to this story is *do not always believe what you are told—you can be anything you see yourself being.* Be inspired about your life and see great things for yourself … you deserve it!

CHAPTER NINE
THE LAW OF ATTRACTION

What we give out, we get back. What goes around comes around. As we think so shall we be. These are all expressions of the law of attraction. This is a law that works whether we believe in it or not. Think back to a time when something happened that you were afraid would happen. How much energy did you waste *not wanting* that thing to happen? How much time did you put into worrying about the experience before you had it? The law of attraction brings to us what we focus on—regardless of whether we want it or not. Period. How many times have you worried about something that eventually happened, and your response was, "I knew it would happen?" Well, congratulations, you got your wish!

The DVD called *The Secret* (www.thesecret.tv) uses the legend of Aladdin and his lamp as a great metaphor. Aladdin finds the lamp, rubs it, and the genie comes out. The genie always says the same thing, "Your wish is my command!" In the movie, the genie represents the universal source that created us all and gives us life. I call this energy God, but there are many names for God so it doesn't really matter what you call it, despite the fact that wars have been fought over terminology for thousands of years and continue today. This energy always gives us whatever we think about most—good or bad. If our thoughts are on how great our lives are, the genie says, "Your wish is my command!" If our thoughts are on how miserable our lives are, the genie says, "Your wish is my command!" It is always the same answer because the universal source does not choose our good or our bad, it simply produces the result, so we continue to get more of what we think about the most.

All day long we are attracting to us, by our thoughts, all kinds of circumstances. If someone says to you, "That outfit makes your look fat," the actual comment takes place in only a few seconds but your reaction to it lasts all day until you can get home and rip those clothes off. Chances are you will never wear them again regardless of how much you like the outfit. When you got dressed at the beginning of the day you must have felt comfortable in it, or you probably would have worn something else. The truth is that the comment most likely had nothing to do with the clothes at all. People make these kinds of comments all the time and we may never really know what their motives are. Maybe they are jealous because they think you look better than they do, or maybe they are the kind of people who feel better about themselves when others are feeling uncomfortable. It could also be that they are in the habit of saying something—anything—just to hear themselves talk and the comment was not intended to make you feel uncomfortable. Maybe there really is no motive at all. But if you buy into comments like these, the law of attraction starts acting upon your feelings, creating more experiences in your day that will make you feel even more uncomfortable. It works like a domino effect: you set up the dominos on end in a row and knock over the first one, and what happens? They all fall. That's why, when we start feeling unsure of ourselves, or as if we are not good enough, experiences start coming at us one after another to prove we are right. Think back to an experience in your own life when this has happened. It happens to everyone until we become aware that *we* are setting ourselves up with our thoughts.

Trust yourself enough to know that whatever you choose to wear is perfect because you are not the clothes you are wearing, you are what's inside. Protect your spirit by not allowing these kinds of comments to make you feel bad about yourself. Of course, clothing is a minor issue compared to many others we may experience, but I hope you get the idea. Anything—big or small—can be handled in the same way. One bad grade on a test you took when you had the flu, an embarrassing moment when you tripped and fell down in front of everyone, the crucial basket you missed at the beginning of the big game. All of these kinds of experiences can start an avalanche of negativity, creating more of the same, if you allow it. Be aware of how you are attracting experiences in your life and choose to be an *active attractor*, conscious of how your thoughts are creating each experience for you. Take charge of your experiences and your life.

In her book, *Excuse Me, Your Life Is Waiting: the astonishing power of feelings*, Lynn Grabhorn tells a story about "Little Slugger Jessie." It's a Little League baseball story that is a wonderful example of the law of attraction. It seems every time Jessie gets up to bat (and the bat is taller than he is), he hits the ball over the fence for a homerun. When asked how he does it, his answer is, "I dunno, each time I get up to bat

I just feel what it's gonna be like to connect, and I do." His *focus* is on hitting the ball.

Look at the people in your life who seem to have everything going for them—success, happiness, and good health. Pay attention to their attitudes. They are always positive, uplifting people, and it *feels good* to be around them. They are living their lives using the law of attraction. It's easy to tell what people are thinking about most of the time by looking at what is working or not working in their lives. The people who talk a lot about prosperity and happiness have it. The people who talk about sickness and lack have that in their lives. We are what we think about most. If we are always thinking about what we don 't have, we are creating more of the same, and we are keeping away the abundance that is just waiting to come into our lives. When you understand this law you will become very careful about what you focus on. Remember the genie? Your wish is my command? Stop yourself when you start to say something negative to your friends. If you have to, say nothing at all until you get into the habit of saying words that will create the life you want.

To turn your life around, take some time each day to write down all the things you are grateful for. There are many things we have to be grateful for even in the worst of times in our lives. Instead of being resentful because you don't have the new clothes you want, be grateful for the clothes you have. Instead of being resentful for the mean things your friends or siblings have said to you, be grateful for the fun times you've had together. Instead of being resentful that your parents spend time working, be grateful for the money they provide to feed and cloth you. Keep a Gratitude Journal and watch your life change. Each night before you go to sleep write down five things that you have been grateful for during the day—there are always at least five things to be grateful for! When you get a good grade on a test write that down. When you felt good in the clothes you wore that day, write that down. When you felt good about helping a friend with their homework, write that down. Even dare to take it a step further. Do what *The Secret* DVD tells you: at the top of a page write *I am so happy and grateful now that ...* and fill in the blank. Be grateful not only for what you already have in your life, but for all the things you want to *create* in your life, and see them as though they already exist. When we take the time to be grateful, more good things happen to us. And that is equally true about our relationships. When we are grateful for the people around us and *see* ourselves having wonderful relationships, our relationships start to change for the better. As we quit complaining about what is wrong and start focusing on what is right, good stuff happens … it's just like magic!

CHAPTER TEN
ENJOY THIS DAY

Your life is happening right now—this is truly the only moment you have! The past is over—including all of the drama you continue to talk about. The future hasn't happened yet—including all of the things you are trying to force to happen right now and all the things you might be worrying about. The present is the only time you have, so *practice being present in your life.* Stop worrying about what might happen and do what you can—in this moment—to *choose* to make what *is happening* the best it can be. Practice being comfortable in your own skin and being proud of who you are. Let me tell you how I have come to understand this process in my life.

I was born to a wonderful mother who loved me and my sister very much. Unfortunately, she married a man who drank excessively, and they both became alcoholics. I was so embarrassed by my mom and stepfather's behavior that I became obsessed with trying to look perfect at all times. I would never leave the house unless my hair and clothes were flawless. In junior high school one day a girl said, "You look like you just stepped out of a magazine!" I thought I had finally achieved my ultimate goal—convincing everyone that my life was OK. I didn't realize it at fourteen years old, but I was setting myself up for a lifetime of unhappiness. I didn't realize how much my obsession to look good was stealing from my life. I didn't realize how much time and energy I was taking *out of my life,* just so I could feel good about me. I could never have looked in the mirror in those days and said, "I love you." I realize now that I didn't even know what loving myself meant. I was too busy trying to be perfect to allow myself to really have fun and enjoy my life.

This obsession continued for over thirty years. When I think back now I have to laugh out loud at some of the habits I fell into. When I first got married and started keeping house I used to wear out a vacuum cleaner in six months. I actually paste waxed and buffed the linoleum floors to such a shine that my children took their little lives in their hands just trying to walk across them without falling. At three years old my son Jeff would be playing in his room and he'd leave for a few minutes to go to the bathroom. When he returned, he'd find his toys put away and his room spotless. He spent a lot of time asking, "Mama, where are my toys?" One of my most vivid memories is of my daughter Janet's fifth birthday. She had beautiful, long brown hair and I insisted that she wear it up in a "bun twisty thing" for her party. Of course, she cried that she didn't want to, but she finally gave in. I guess she had been my child long enough to know—everything had to be perfect. The moment the last child left the party she said, "Oĸ mama, take my hair down now." Today I realize that she spent her entire party hating her hair.

I didn't own a pair of jeans until I was over thirty years old—they were just too casual! There were countless times when I sat on the floor in front of my closet and cried because I had nothing to wear—even though the closet was, of course, full. I could fill a book with all the weird stuff I thought was important over the years, but my point is this: give yourselves a break and learn to be comfortable in your own skin. That is the greatest gift we can give ourselves—to be comfortable in our own skin. Think about what it might feel like to enter a room filled with teenagers you don't know and be totally comfortable. Or give a presentation in your classroom feeling confident and at peace.

We've all felt uncomfortable in our own skins. We've felt self conscious and worried that someone will talk about us or stare at us. Remember, we are all on this earth to *enjoy life.* That means to look forward to each day, be comfortable in it, and see it as an adventure. Learn to relax and not take life so seriously. The truth is that most people won't remember what clothes you were wearing or what your hair looked like on any particular day. What they do remember is if you had a smile on your face and were fun to be around. You all know people who are "perfect" in every way—weight, clothes, looks, makeup—and yet it's not fun to be around them because they are such high maintenance. Everything is all about them. They talk, talk, talk about themselves. Then, on the other hand, you all know people who are not so perfect by some people's standards but who always have smiles on their faces and seem comfortable being who they are. You find that you love to be around them. They always seem to light up the room when they walk in. Be happy and confident in who you are. Your confidence in yourself will increase your friend's confidence in you. Relax, smile and have some fun.

Many years ago my group of girlfriends would plan weekend trips together. Most of us would bring large suitcases and take everything we owned so we would always look perfect—and we'd have to lug those suitcases all over the place. My friend Ann took only a small duffle bag. She was one of those people who would light up the room when she entered, not by her clothing, but by her smile and wonderful attitude. In fact, she might have been wearing a pair of shorts and wrinkled t-shirt but no one ever noticed, including us. To this day, Ann is one of the greatest examples in my life of people who are comfortable in their own skins.

Ask yourself what is the first thing you think about when you wake up in the morning. Do you look forward to the day or do you start thinking about everything that is wrong in your life? Do you look forward to going to school and seeing your friends or do you start running all your drama through your mind as you take your shower? When you get dressed, are you dressing for you, choosing something that really *feels good*, or are you dressing for everyone else at school? Are you calm in the mornings or do you rush around and stress yourself out? If you lean toward the negative side of any of these questions, ask yourself, "Why?" You can create your day with your thoughts. You are in control, so take charge of your life by learning to enjoy it. Don't cheat yourself out of a single day of happiness. Be responsible for the thoughts you think, and create a day you can be proud of. The more good days you create, the better you feel about your life—and the better your life becomes. Remember the genie … "Your wish is my command!"

One of the ways you can tell if you are truly at ease and enjoying life is to look at yourself in photographs. A picture is worth a thousand words. If you force a smile, the falseness shows in a picture. There's a strained look on your face. If you think back to when the photo was taken, you probably realize you weren't truly enjoying yourself, or you had something on your mind. In other photos you can almost see the sparkle in your eyes, and you know you were probably feeling really good. I have found that taking deep breaths when I feel tension is a wonderful and easy way to release stress. It also allows you to relax and feel comfortable. Next time you are posing for a picture, take a deep breath, feel yourself *smiling from the inside*, and create a feeling of butterflies in your stomach. Then look at the picture of yourself and see the difference in your smile and the look on your face.

Someone once said, "There are two kinds of people in this life … those who walk into a room and say, 'Here I am!' and those who walk into a room and say, 'Ahh … there you are!'" When you are truly interested in your friends, you attract and keep more of them. Everyone, including you, wants to be around friends who make them feel good. What kind of friend do you want to be?

CHAPTER ELEVEN
THE JOY OF DRIVING

I can still remember the first time I got behind the wheel of a car—*by myself*—and felt the joy of having a real driver's license. What an exhilarating feeling that was to be so free and independent. How proud I felt to be old enough to drive—without Mom watching every move! While driving is a wonderful feeling of independence, it is also a great responsibility. When you get behind the wheel of a car, you are not only taking responsibility for the safety of yourself and anyone in your car, but the responsibility to be a courteous driver to everyone else on the roads you travel. I know that sounds like a lot of responsibility and might just make you want to put your car keys in the dresser drawer (yeah, right!) but the purpose of this chapter is not to scare you to death, but to ask you to be *totally present* when you are driving. It's easy to become distracted at any age, but especially so when you are just learning to drive and have so many new skills and experiences to learn all at the same time.

I live in a small town in the northern California foothills, so the traffic is nothing like you might see in large cities or suburbs. Nevertheless, there have been several accidents lately on the highways near my home that have taken the lives of great kids and adults.

While driving, a simple thing like answering a cell phone, changing a CD, or reaching to pick up your sunglasses can cause anyone of any age to lose control of a car. A simple swerve can aim you directly into oncoming traffic. Even a simple merge, as a road changes from two lanes to one, can create disaster when there is no place to get out of the way. That situation caused a horrible and devastating accident the day before graduation last year, which is what prompted me to add this chapter to the book. Two brothers were driving home from school, approaching a place in the road where two lanes merged into one. Evidently, the boys' car was beside another car, and both drivers apparently thought they could go first and get out of the way of the other. The result was a spinout that sent the boys' car into oncoming traffic, killing both of them as well as a woman in one of the oncoming cars. All of these precious people were so loved in our community that the pain was felt by literally thousands. It will take a long time for the hearts of the families and friends of these wonderful people to heal. We never think it can happen to us, yet in a brief moment the joyful anticipation of graduating from high school turned into widespread sadness.

A car is a wonderful invention and has certainly given us a lot of freedom. We all simply need to be totally in the *present* when driving, and pay total attention to the other cars and the world around us. It's also helpful to use the power of visualization. Each time I get into my car, before I even start the engine, I visualize myself driving down the road to my destination and arriving safely. Several times during the trip I visualize white light around each of the tires and a bubble of white light around the entire car (please don't visualize so much that you forget to pay attention to your driving!). As I am driving and I go through green lights I say, "Thank you, God," and, surprisingly enough, I almost always have green lights! When I see someone pulling in front of me I back off so there is plenty of room. If someone is following close behind me I pull into the slow lane and let them go by. I do not choose to lose any energy trying to figure out why someone is following so close, I simply assume there must be some sort of an emergency.

This is how I drive *now*! Let me tell you how I *used* to drive. There was a time when I gave everyone who followed too close behind me the "brake test." I would hit my brakes several times in a row until the driver got the idea that I was not happy with the way he was driving. I used to get angry and allow everyone's poor driving habits to upset my life. It was easy to find people to get mad at in those days because that's where my focus was—and you get what you focus on, remember? Well, one day I got a speeding ticket for going 50 in a 35-mile zone. Since I'd always had a perfect driving record, I chose to go to traffic school instead of having a flaw on my record. I am convinced that was the best thing that ever happened to me. Living in a small town, I was given the option of watching videos at home and taking a test rather than taking an actual class. I thought that would be great because I was sure I could fast forward to get the answers and not even watch the video. Boy, was I surprised! The people who put those videos together are pretty smart. It was impossible to take the test without watching the video. So, I sat down to watch. That's the day I changed the way I drove for good.

The things I saw in that video of real-life situations took my breath away. There were accounts of people on the freeway who were victims of (my favorite) "brake test." But in these situations, the "test" inspired road rage—they shot people, stabbed people, and dragged people from their cars and beat them up for doing the same thing I'd been doing for years. There were many other causes of road rage in that video, and I realized very quickly how easy it would be to become one of the statistics. You never know what will set another person off—and driving seems to bring out the worst in people.

Never take the position of needing to be right when it comes to driving. Choose to be the one who backs off and creates room for the other car. Choose to be the one who allows other people to merge onto the freeway safely. Choose to be the one who stays in a peaceful state if someone cuts you off. Choose to be the one who allows another car to go first at a stop sign. Choose to drive the speed limit, peacefully. Remember, there is no place for *ego* when it comes to driving. When you are behind the wheel of a car there is never anything to prove. Driving is a privilege and needs to be taken very seriously. *Your life depends on it!*

CHAPTER TWELVE
THE GIFT OF GIVING

Everyone, at some point in life, experiences the joy of giving. It might be as simple as giving one of your toys to another child when you are little, or part of your sandwich to a friend at school. When this experience takes place, there is a place within us that *feels good* because we are willing to give.

I have a sticker on the inside of my shower door that I see every morning. It says, *Today I take time to practice small acts of kindness.* I have it there as a reminder that giving makes me feel good—it literally makes my heart smile. I know from my own experiences that the greatest gift we can give *ourselves* is to be willing to give *of ourselves* to help others feel good. If we pay attention, there are many opportunities each day to practice small acts of kindness, even if it's simply giving a smile to someone who needs one. The next time you are tempted to ignore someone at school who doesn't quite *fit in*, give him a sincere smile instead and notice the look on his face—you will have made his day, and it cost you nothing. The next time you're at the grocery store and a mother with a cranky child is behind you in line, let her go first. When you're at a department store and an older person—who may have difficulty standing—drops something, help them pick it up. If a sales clerk is having a bad day, choose to be kind and watch her mood change. There are so many ways each and every day to practice being kind to others that cost you absolutely nothing and give you so much in return.

One day during the Christmas rush my daughter and I were making a purchase at the mall. It was obvious that the sales clerk was not feeling well. I asked her if she was OK and she said she was sick but couldn't afford to go home. She said that, even though it was toward the end of the day, she would loose $12 if she left early. She said, "I know $12 doesn't seem like very much, but it makes a big difference at the end of the week when I try to pay my bills." I handed her a $20 bill and told her that I wanted to give her the option to leave early if she chose and not feel like she had to continue working for the money when she was ill.

The look on her face—that a stranger would give her money—said it all. I don't know if she left early or not, but the joy I felt in giving her the option was a gift to *me* that truly made my day. When we focus on helping others, the focus is turned away from our problems, and we feel much better about ourselves.

In his book, *Inspiration*, Dr. Wayne W. Dyer says, "Practice being generous as often as you can. Promise yourself to extend some kind of unexpected generosity to someone, preferably a stranger, every single day for two weeks." I believe that is the best advice a person could give or get. When we put our attention on what we can do for others, the good in our own lives continues to increase. Remember the law of attraction? What we put out into the world, we get back. Choosing to give of our time, talent, and treasure is a wonderful way to create increased good in our own lives and the lives of others—it is the way life works. Take some time today to think of ways you can help others over the next two weeks. It will make you feel so good I bet you'll make it into a habit that will last a lifetime. And, receiving a random act of kindness often inspires the recipient to return the "favor" to another stranger—imagine the possibilities!

About fifteen years ago I took a twelve-week class at church called the 4T Prosperity Program. During the twelve weeks, as part of the program, it was suggested that we tithe 10 percent of our income to the church. That was a great challenge for me because, at that time, I had the idea that if I gave that much of my income there would not be enough to pay my bills. But, I made the *commitment* to tithe, and the result is still amazing to me today. During that time I lived in north Lake Tahoe and managed one of the offices for a short-term, vacation-rental business. In addition to running the office, my job was to put new properties on the rental program. I took the prosperity class at church during the slowest months of the year for adding new properties. To my surprise, each week my secretary would say over and over, "There's another owner on the phone wanting to put his rental property on the program … what are you doing?" She knew the odds of getting any new properties at that time were slim to none. At our weekly sales meetings, the managers of the other three offices were totally amazed and, when I told them it was the 4T Prosperity Program, they all laughed. It really didn't matter to me whether they believed the program worked or not, because at the end of the twelve weeks I had thirty new properties signed up. I didn't know it at the time, but this class was an example of the law of attraction.

Today, I contribute money to many wonderful organizations that help others. One of my favorites is the Christian Children's Fund. I sponsor a six-year-old boy named Isaac David who lives in Ecuador. It makes my heart smile that he is able to go to school because of my monthly donation. His mother has sent pictures of him in his pre-school class. He is one of the older children because his family could not afford the uniforms and tuition until they received a sponsor. We correspond regularly and it is a joy to see the pride that is so obvious in his pictures. This joy in my heart costs only $24 a month. The same $24 we spend on one dinner can send a child to school for a month and change a life. For less than the cost of an iPod, we can pay for an entire year of schooling.

St. Jude's Children's Hospital is another organization that I have contributed to for over fifteen years. I started with a small monthly donation and have increased it over the years as my income grew. They do so much good for children with cancer and, through donations, no child is ever sent away because of lack of money. Even the families are supported so they can stay with their children through the treatment process.

Heifer International is an organization that is helping people help themselves all over the world. Susan Sarandon was on Oprah's TV show one day and explained how she had bought a goat for a family in Uganda ten years ago. In that family was an eight-year-old girl who desperately wanted to go to school, but her family could not afford to send her. The goat changed her life. In fact, she walked out on stage to join Oprah and Susan, wearing her beautiful native costume. When she said she was now eighteen years old and attending university, I was sold. The cost for donating a goat includes enough additional money to train the family to care for the animal so it will survive, give milk (which improves the health of the family), and have offspring. The agreement is that the family can sell the extra milk, but they have to give one of the offspring to another family in the village. As time goes on, they not only have milk to sell, but they have other goats to sell, too. In time, one little goat can change the lives of an entire village. As we help others help themselves, we will change the world. As the old proverb says, feed a man a fish and he eats for a day, teach a man to fish and he eats for a lifetime.

A few years ago there was a documentary on television called *Ryan's Well*. It was about a young Canadian boy who collected money to provide wells in some villages in Uganda. He made a huge difference in the lives of many people when he was only a first grader in the small town of Kemptville, Ontario. Ryan Hreljac wanted the people of Africa to have clean drinking water, so he started a campaign that ended up raising over a million dollars—and he didn't stop there. Visit the Web site for Ryan's Well Foundation at www.ryanswell.ca to see what a six-year-old can accomplish with a little inspiration.

Make this day the day you decide to make a difference in someone else's life. Volunteer at a retirement home. Older people love to have young people around—it gives them someone to talk to and brings back memories of their youth—and all it costs is your time. If you sing, get other kids who sing and perform for them. Or play board games with them, or read aloud—the ideas are endless. Get some of your friends together and form a club to help others. You will be surprised at all the great ideas you can come up with as a group. Find a cause like Ryan did and make a difference in people's lives. Use your imagination and *see the good you can do for others.* Then bring your plan to life and pay attention to how *you* feel. The act of helping others is the greatest gift we can give to ourselves. When our spirits feel good, our lives are filled with wonderful, happy days.

CHAPTER THIRTEEN
MEDITATION AND BREATH

Meditation is not something weird that has to be done a certain way. And it also is not difficult. There are no particular rules you have to follow in order for meditation to be effective in increasing focus and eliminating stress. It is simply a process of getting quiet and relaxing your mind ... you know the one that has 60,000 thoughts a day?

My granddaughters found it humorous for years when they would see me meditating. When they were younger and meditation was mentioned in a conversation, they would say, "This is Grandma ..." then they'd plop down on the floor and sit in a meditative pose with hands on knees—complete with thumb and index finger touching. My older granddaughter, when she was about five years old, used to put my headset on and listen to guided meditation tapes. It was pretty comical to see her little head bobbing as she tried to stay awake while sitting up—yes, in meditative pose!

I was reading a newsletter recently from Dr. Deepak Chopra and Dr. David Simon that offered a wonderful and easy meditation practice. It's called the *So Hum* meditation. All you do is sit in a chair comfortably and close your eyes. Take a slow deep breath through your nose as you think the word "so." Exhale slowly through your nose while thinking the word "hum." Continue breathing naturally and easily, silently repeating "so" and "hum" for twenty minutes. Make this an effortless and simple process. When the time is up, continue to sit quietly, with your eyes closed, for a few minutes. If you will take some time each day to do this one simple practice, you will notice a calmness that has been missing in your life of computers and cell phones.

The best times to meditate are shortly after awakening in the morning and again in the later afternoon or early evening. The morning meditation starts your day with a calm mental attitude, and the later session helps calm your mind after your day's activity. When you finish the meditation in the morning, *visualize* your day the way you would like it to be. See your day filled with wonderful experiences. If you are having a test, see yourself getting a good grade. See your experiences with your friends and the other people you come into contact with during the day as peaceful, kind, and fun. Take the time to create the day you would like to have instead of thinking about all the things you don't want to happen. Good experiences come from good thoughts—and good thoughts are encouraged when you feel peaceful inside.

Dr. Wayne W. Dyer has a wonderful meditation book and CD called *Getting in the Gap* that has helped many people reach that still, peaceful place within. It's another easy way to create peace in your life. You can find this book and CD at most of the popular bookstores, or on Dr. Dyer's Web site www.drwaynedyer.com.

If you are willing to do a little research on meditation, you will find that it is not some far out practice that only yogis do in a certain pose for hours on end. Meditation is one of the greatest gifts we can give ourselves, and it costs nothing but our willingness to sit quietly for a short time each day. Sitting on a rock and watching the ocean is a form of meditation. So is staring at a crackling fire in the fireplace or watching a sunset. Anything that causes your mind to relax is a form of meditation. I guarantee that once you give yourself the gift of quiet time, you will notice less drama in your life. Pretty soon the challenges stop coming your way and you can't remember the last time something went wrong or you complained about anything. You begin to notice how calm you feel and how peaceful your breathing has become. Now, isn't that result worth a few minutes of your time each day?

Breath is life, yet it is one of the things most of us don't even think about. Without breath we would literally not be here. Most people go through their entire lives being unconscious of the breath that keeps them alive—we don't get up in the morning and say "OK, I have to breathe in and out all day." We just breathe. That's one of the many functions that our glorious bodies automatically take care of for us. Because it is so automatic, we don't think much about it at all, but the *way* we breathe has a big affect on our bodies.

Start paying attention to the way you breathe throughout your day. Most of us are shallow breathers, especially when we are in what we consider to be a stressful situation. When we breathe shallowly, our chests go up and down and our breaths are short. This actually deprives our bodies of the oxygen we need for optimum health. And we need extra oxygen to help reduce the stressful feeling. Practice breathing from your abdomen, not your chest—that's where deep breathing comes from. As you take in a breath watch your abdomen go out. And as you exhale watch you abdomen go in. This is just the opposite of how most people breathe. Practice breathing. As you go through your day be conscious of how you breathe. When you notice yourself taking shallow breaths, stop and begin breathing from your abdomen. This is a simple change that will do wonders for your health and your peace of mind—and you can do it "secretly" at anytime throughout your day.

Become Happy in 8 Minutes: Simple, Powerful Steps to Improve Your Mood—Quickly! is a wonderful book written by Siimon Reynolds. In his chapter on breathing he says, "If you breathe only with your chest, you must take about three times as many breaths to get the same amount of air as a deep abdominal breath would give you. If each abdominal breath gives you about three times more oxygen, imagine what a difference breathing that way can make to your health over a lifetime." His book is informative and written with humor. It contains chapters that he calls "minutes", describing easy ways to create happiness in your life. It takes about an hour to read this book, but the information Siimon offers is priceless.

CHAPTER FOURTEEN
ARE YOU MEAN OR KIND?

Most of you have probably seen the movie *Mean Girls*. If you have, I hope it made you stop and think about how kids can treat each other. My granddaughter was a varsity cheerleader for her high school. One Friday night I sat in the bleachers at the football game in front of about twenty teenagers who were *supposed* to be friends. During the entire two hours that I sat there I noticed there weren't many nice comments coming from the group, and lots of negative, critical comments were slung back and forth. There was one boy's voice that I heard over and over above the crowd who spent the entire time doing his best to embarrass the other kids … especially the girls. I noticed that the other kids took his treatment rather than call him on it, and I believe I know why. This kind of person has gotten away with this kind of "attitude" for so long that if someone did call him on it he most likely would respond by embarrassing them even more until they eventually left the group to crawl under a rock somewhere. My questions to you are, Why would you let anyone treat you so disrespectfully? Why would you purposely do that to anyone else? This guy continues to do what he does because he always gets away with it. It's his way of keeping the rest of his "friends" on the defensive so they don't direct the same kind of abuse toward him. As long as he is the bully with the loudest mouth and the strongest opinions, no one will embarrass him and force him to look for that rock to crawl under!

As the *Mean Girls* movie shows quite well, girls can be awful. Girls have created so much competition among each other—looks, clothes, possessions, grades and popularity. I say *created* because everyone has the choice at any moment to be happy, kind, and content with themselves and others. If you think the only way you can be popular is by making other kids afraid of *crossing* you so you won't embarrass them—what kind of friendship is that? You will become more popular being kind than being mean.

At every school there are bullies who love to make other kids' lives miserable. They love to find something—anything—to hold against someone that they decide they don't like so they can convince others to dislike that person, too. It's time to break the cycle. Don't allow yourself to go to school one more day stressed out because of what someone might say to you. Be happy with yourself and refuse to be friends with someone who is treating you with disrespect. If you don't remember anything else from this book, please remember this: "We teach people how to treat us by what we're willing to accept." You don't have to fight back, simply make a new choice. Do you realize that bullies are the minority? For every bully there are hundreds of kids who are kind to each other. Seek those people out and choose to be friends with people you feel good around. Also, don't be so quick to jump on the band wagon when someone talks badly about another kid—because *you* could be the one they decide to talk about next. Always decide for yourself who you want to be friends with based on how people treat you, not on someone else's opinion. Give people a chance. Look for the good in everyone—see what's right about people instead of what's wrong.

I received an e-mail recently that really made me think about this subject. It was about a teacher who asked her students to list the names of the other students in the room on two sheets of paper, leaving a space between each name. Then she asked them to think of the *nicest* thing they could say about each classmate and write it down under the name. The students handed in their papers, and that weekend the teacher wrote down the name of each student on an individual sheet of paper and listed what everyone in the class had said about him or her. On Monday she gave all the students their own lists and asked them to read them. Before long the entire class was smiling. She heard comments like "Really!" "I never knew I meant anything to anyone," and "I didn't know anyone liked me so much!" No one ever mentioned those papers in class again and she never knew if they discussed them after class or with their parents, but it didn't matter because the exercise had accomplished its purpose. The students were happy with themselves and with each other—they were friends.

I hope you will use this story to think about the nice things you can say about your friends. Focus on their good points. Tell your friends what you like about them—even the mean kids, because your example might have the power to encourage them to change from being mean to being kind. The one sure way to create kindness in your relationships is to ask yourself, "Would I ever want someone to say mean things to embarrass me?" The answer is always, "No!" so don't be willing to do it to anyone else.

CHAPTER FIFTEEN
THE AGREEMENTS WE MAKE

Several years ago don Miguel Ruiz wrote a book called *The Four Agreements: A Practical Guide to Personal Freedom, A Toltec Wisdom Book*. It is one of the many books that have changed the way people live their lives. Don Miguel was born to a family of healers in rural Mexico. He attended medical school, and later he taught medicine and practiced as a surgeon (www.miguelruiz.com).

We come into this world as little children with an open mind. During our growing up years we accept opinions—agreements—from other people. These agreements either help us have a peaceful life or cause us to have a life filled with unhappiness.

Use your own life as an example and try to remember a time in your life when you have agreed with something someone told you that did not create a positive result. We all, at some point in our lives, believe that other people have the answers for us and take the information in as our own. Many times there is a helpful positive result, and those times are valuable to us—like not touching the stove because it is hot, or not running into the street when a car is coming. There are other times, though, when what we experience may not be as good for us— like assuming other people are out to get us or being offended by what others say and do.

Here are don Miguel's four agreements: be impeccable with your word, don't take anything personally, don't make assumptions, and always do your best.

To be impeccable with your word means to be aware of what you say and to understand that with each word you speak you are creating your life. Your word can be the sweetest thing you could ever say to some-one or it can be the most hurtful. Your words can create a beautiful experience or they can destroy everything around you, and it is your choice. An extreme example is how Hitler used his words to create fear in the people of Germany and got them to do the most terrible things to each other. Another example is the holocaust in Rwanda that I spoke about in another chapter, where people were convinced—over the radio—to kill one million people.

Being impeccable with your word is the most powerful of all the agreements because when you really pay attention to the words you speak, you realize why your life is working the way it is. If you take this one agreement and make a commitment to yourself to say only positive and kind things to yourself and others, your life experiences will start to change. As you get better and better at catching yourself *before* you say something that will hurt yourself or someone else, you eventually stop having those thoughts altogether. It is really pretty amazing what happens—there comes a day when you hear something that you might have said in the past and realize that it is not even a thought to you anymore. It gives you a feeling of pride that you have become a better person than you used to be.

Start today to *listen to yourself* and refuse to allow unkind words to come out of your mouth any longer. And if they slip out once in a while, don't beat yourself up—say to yourself, "That's not my truth," and be more aware next time. Refuse to contribute to the gossip at school and refuse to allow yourself to take it personally or be offended if someone is gossiping about you.

When something happens in our lives that doesn't feel good, the first thing most of us do is take it personally. When we take it personally we become offended and our first reaction is to defend ourselves—which creates conflict. Most of the time, when we are taking something personally, it is really just someone else's opinion of what we should do and really has nothing to do with us. Be willing to get rid of the word *should* and change it to *could*—"should" is what we think we or someone else *needs* to do and "could" is what we *choose* to do.

We all grow up in the world with our own agreements and, depending upon those agreements, we develop opinions of how the world "should" work. If you have an agreement with yourself that your boyfriend should call you every night and he doesn't—you most likely will take it personally, wondering if he really likes you. The truth may be that your boyfriend simply doesn't know you like to be called every night. So, instead of taking it personally, change your agreement with yourself. Don't use a phone call to determine whether he likes you or not. Getting along with others in this world includes letting them be who they are. When you quit making a phone call so important, he may call more often ... remember the law of attraction?

When you feel good, everything around you is good. When you feel sad, everything around you is sad. There are really only two core choices—thoughts of *fear* or *love*. There are only those two agreements for everything that happens in our lives. If we are living in fear—don't feel good about ourselves—and someone says something to us that we don't agree with, we will take it personally and get angry. If we are living in love—feel good about who we are—and someone says the same thing to us, we will not be offended. If you choose to take things personally you are literally giving other people power to control your happiness. When you change your agreement and stop taking what other people say to you personally, you will be at peace, and the interesting thing is that people quit trying to upset you. If you don't react, there is no need for them to bother—they will move on to someone else.

Have you ever heard some gossip that upset you and, when you repeated it to people you felt *should* have been upset about it, they weren't? They were using this agreement to *not take things personally*. They may have had good reason to get upset, but by not taking the comment personally they were able to remain at peace. This is a great example of choosing your battles and knowing that you don't have to participate in one if you don't want to.

When you take things personally you are setting yourself up to suffer for nothing. Sometimes we are so attached to the drama that is created by taking things personally that we even help each other suffer. How many times have you or your friends kept a problem alive by talking about it over and over. You might as well put signs on your back that say "kick me" because that's what is happening to your spirit when you continue to be offended and upset. Most of the time, if you refuse to take things personally, you will see that they are really not personal after all—you are making an assumption of what the another person is thinking. Many times people say things without thinking or being conscious of how their words affect others.

I have been guilty of making assumptions and have noticed over the years that more often than not the assumptions were not correct—and caused needless problems in my life. The problem with making assumptions is that we believe the assumption is the truth. When we make an *assumption* we also take it *personally* and create unnecessary drama in our lives. I'm willing to bet that most of the sadness and drama you have experienced in your life has been caused by either making assumptions or taking things personally—or both.

We create unhappiness by making assumptions, taking things personally, and gossiping about our assumptions to others. Always ask questions if you are wondering about something—because assumptions set us up for unhappiness. Sometimes our assumptions are more like fantasies. We believe someone likes us and we develop a whole relationship in our minds—only to find out the other person doesn't feel the same. We get hurt and don't realize that, if we had been unwilling to make the assumption in the first place, the whole thing would not have happened—we would have saved ourselves the pain. If you are in a relationship, don't assume the other person always knows what you want. Be willing to communicate your feelings. The only way to really get to know someone is by sharing thoughts and feelings. Becoming aware of your habit of making assumptions and understanding how much damage it does in your life is a major step to changing the habit for good. Watch yourself when you are tempted to make an assumption, and refuse to fall into the trap. Create the new habit of asking questions and gathering information that you need to know the truth.

And make it a habit to always do your best. Your best will be different in the morning when you are feeling refreshed from a good night's sleep than it might be in the evening when you have spent two hours doing homework. Do your best and you will never feel like you have to judge yourself for not being good enough. Knowing you are always doing your best in any situation enables you to relax and complete any project in a peaceful state—whether it is a homework assignment or sport activity. Don't push yourself to be better than anyone else, just be the best *you* are capable of being *in the moment*.

When we do things just for the reward—getting recognition or a material prize—we miss the point of doing our best. We don't enjoy what we're doing under these conditions so we usually don't do our best. We also look for reasons to blame others if our experience is not a pleasant one—creating resentment and judgments. On the other hand, if you enjoy what you're doing, just for the sake of doing it, it's usually more fun. Doing our best is an agreement we can have with ourselves that we can feel good about. No matter what the grade is on the test or the score is in the game—our reward is that we know we did our best! When we know who we are and are proud of who we are—regardless of the outcome—then doing our best doesn't feel like work. If we like what we do, if we are always doing our best, then we will begin to really enjoy our lives.

I have made an agreement with myself that I love to read. There was a time in my life that I believed just the opposite. In those days I would sit down to read, immediately start feeling tired, and put the book down. Changing this one agreement created a new habit for me that changed my life—and, in the process, created this book.

Don't allow old agreements and self-limiting beliefs to rob you of joy in your life and create needless suffering. Develop positive agreements in your life, and *do your best* to keep these agreements. If you find yourself in the middle of drama, use one of these agreements to put your life back into perspective and get back on track. We have all spent years creating the habits that are not working in our lives—give yourself some time to make the changes. Be aware when you slip, and realize how much better your life works when you use positive agreements.

CHAPTER SIXTEEN
WHAT IS LIFE?

Have you ever wondered what life is really all about? I don't think I asked myself that question in my teenage years, but my teenage years were not as challenging as yours seem to be today—so in case you have had that thought, I offer you my interpretation.

What is our purpose? Do you think it is to get up each day, eat breakfast, go to school, come home, do homework, spend time on the Internet, text message on your cell phone, eat dinner, watch a video, go to bed, and then do it all over the next day? That is what most of us believe, including me for a good portion of my life.

I have learned that there is much more to life than we think. Have you ever asked yourself, "Is this all there is?" Well, if you have, I am happy to say the answer is, "No!" What we see on the surface of our lives, in combination with the habits we create for ourselves, is not all there is. Life is meant to be a miraculous experience. We are given the opportunity to create our lives any way we choose. The gift of life is a blessing and the opportunity to create it is something we need to take seriously *and* take responsibility for.

As we've discussed in many of the previous chapters, life is created with our *thoughts*, the *choices* we make, our *intentions*, and what we *visualize* happening in our lives. God gives us free will, and it is that *free will* that sometimes gets us into trouble. God allows us to make choices and think for ourselves, so living as though *this is all there is* and *my life is controlled by my circumstances or other people* robs us of so many wonderful opportunities just waiting to materialize in our lives. Things like happiness! I'm talking about *real happiness* here, not one or two happy moments when things go your way. No—*real happiness*: When nothing anyone says or does can make you angry. When you wake up in the morning and you are happy to be alive—not because you have a new outfit or some other new material thing—just because you are *YOU*. I don't mean this from an ego standpoint—that you're better than anyone else—I am talking about being truly proud of who you are because you *know* you are being the very best person you can possible be—to yourself and others. Being proud of yourself is so important. When you are proud of who you are, it just doesn't matter what anyone else thinks about you. You know you are a good person. Opinions from others don't upset you anymore, and an amazing thing happens: people stop giving you negative opinions when you have a good opinion of yourself.

I had to laugh out loud one day when my granddaughter reacted to the advice I gave her about a problem she had at school with another student. Someone had said something that had hurt her. When I told her to be proud of who she is and not to take it personally if someone says something mean, she looked at me and said, "Grandma, you just don't understand because no one ever says those things to you, your life is fine." I want you all to know that I have had many of the same experiences you are having in your lives and I would bet most of your parents have, too. What I am trying to teach you here is that when you quit *reacting* to these experiences they stop happening. The information in this book comes from direct experience, not from wishful thinking. I have lived this stuff and it works!

This may sound strange to some of you because you may never have felt *real happiness* in your lives—at least not yet. But you can at any moment you choose. Start putting your attention on how you *feel* about yourself, and if you find reasons to put yourself down, or feel you are not good enough, cute enough, thin enough, smart enough, or if any other negative feelings pop up … stop it! You are a child of God. How much better could it get? Until you feel good about yourself, all the material things you could ever get will only bring brief moments of happiness.

Years ago I had a wall hanging that said, "Life is what happens while we're busy making other plans." I believe each of us comes into this life not by accident but on purpose to contribute our gift to this world. Take some time to think about what you may be able to contribute to the world. What is it? It is whatever you are passionate about.

My granddaughter, Jerri, is passionate about journalism. She is the layout editor of her high school newspaper, and writes articles for the paper each week. She graduates from high school this year and her major in college will be journalism. There is no doubt in her mind (or mine) that she will be a Pulitzer Prize winner some day. My younger granddaughter, Delanie, has always been excellent at cheerleading and gymnastics. When she was a very little girl she could do routines as well as the professionals. These are two sports that can cause injuries rather easily. I have watched her on the football field after an injury, and she continues her routine as if nothing had happened. She is so passionate about the sport that she doesn't even feel the pain in the moment.

If you love to draw, take an art class at school. If you love to write, take a creative writing class or journalism class. If you have the gift of making things with your hands, take woodshop. If you love to help people, consider being a teacher and take classes to reach that goal. Pay attention to what you love to do, keep it alive in your heart, and you will end up living a life that is not only rewarding and peaceful but filled with happiness. When we are doing what we love to do, our lives work. Do you have a list of goals you want to reach in your life? Put *happiness* at the top of the list and watch everything else fall into place, because happiness comes from inside of us—it is something we contribute *to* this world.

Life is also intended to be prosperous, and you are never too young to start creating prosperity in every area of your life. Being prosperous is not just about money, although that is part of it because money is really a tool to use for our comfort on this earth. Money is just paper—the value is what we put on it. Generations ago, people bartered with each other. They would trade one product or service for another that they needed to survive. If one farmer grew corn and another grew wheat they would trade with each other so they both would have corn and wheat—but you already know that from your history books. So let's talk about the green stuff. Money is exchanged today for products that we need and, we get money for working … unless we have a money tree in the backyard.

The real purpose of money is to circulate it. Money is energy like everything else in the world—including us. When we earn money; buy food, clothes, or gas for the car; get a haircut; go to the movies; and all the other things we do, money circulates for the good of all. The stores stay in business, people have jobs, and everyone prospers. When we stop treating money like it is something that comes to some and not to others, when we stop feeling jealous because someone has more money than we do, the energy of money changes for us. Remember, everything we focus on we create in our lives. If we are feeling like we don't have enough money, we get more of what we are thinking about … not enough money!

In my own life, when I stopped worrying about how to pay the bills and started *seeing* them paid and being grateful for having the money to pay them, I always had enough money. While a lot of people go online to pay their bills, I still physically make out the checks each month to pay my mortgage and other accounts because I have a *smiley face* on my checks along with the words, "Change your thinking, change your life!" and I want to share that message with the people who have trusted me to pay my bills. There have been times in my life when sitting down to pay the bills has caused stress and fear, but since I have starting using the law of attraction and concentrating on being grateful for what I already have, there is always enough—enough money, time, good health, and prosperity in every area of my life.

Whatever you choose to do in life, do it as a service to others. Want for others what you want for yourself. When you do a job, be happy to do it whether it is a chore around the house or you are working for someone else. Do the best you are capable of doing so you can be proud of the job you have done; see it as a service to others and you will create peace and prosperity in your life. Peace in our world will come when we bring peace to ourselves. We need to find peace within ourselves to make a difference in world peace. Choose to go into your life each day as a *peace maker*—looking for ways to bring peace to yourself and others, and watch how *one* person *can* make a difference. I believe that's what life is all about.

CHAPTER SEVENTEEN
ALWAYS REMEMBER ...
LIFE IS GOOD

Listen to your heart. If something feels good, pay attention to it and see where it fits into your life for your highest good. Be open to new experiences and beware of feeling that you are an "expert" in anything. You cannot learn if you are convinced you already know.

I am amazed at all the information that is available to help us make our lives work. There are hundreds of books and CDs on almost every subject imaginable. If you ask people who you consider have succeeded in their lives, they will almost always mention someone who influenced them along the way. We all have teachers in our lives and, if we pay attention, they are not always who we expect them to be. So treat everyone you meet as the most important person you'll meet each day—you never know what you have to learn from them.

Really succeeding in life is not measured by how much money you make. It is measured by how much *joy* you bring to your life every day. Successful people who are balanced in their lives—work, family, spirituality, and quiet time—do create money, but it seems the money comes best when the focus is on helping others.

I heard a story once about two shoe salesmen who went to the Far East to sell shoes. After three days the first salesman called the home office and said, "I'm taking the next plane home—no prospects here, everyone goes barefoot." After seven days the second salesman called the home office and said, "I have fifty orders—prospects unlimited, nobody here has shoes!" How much success we have is determined by our perception. The second salesman saw an opportunity to supply people with something that they didn't have—shoes—and in the process he became a success. His focus was on helping others.

One of my favorite quotes is by Henry David Thoreau, "If you advance confidently in the direction of your dreams and endeavor to live the life which you have imagined, you will meet with success unexpected in common hours." I believe his message is to pay attention to what makes your heart smile—*live the life that you have imagined.* When you pay attention to what makes *your heart smile* you notice that it always feels good. It also never hurts anyone else because what truly makes your heart smile is always for the highest good of all.

In her book *A Return to Love: Reflections on the Principles of A Course In Miracles*, Marianne Williamson says, "Our Deepest Fear is not that we are inadequate. Our deepest fear is that we are powerful beyond measure. It is our light, not our darkness that most frightens us. We ask ourselves, Who am I to be brilliant, gorgeous, talented, fabulous? Actually, who are you *not* to be? You are a child of God. Your playing small does not serve the world. There is nothing enlightened about shrinking so that other people won't feel insecure around you ..."

What sort of things do you think make us feel *less than fabulous?* If we are honest with ourselves, it is usually the little things that are really not important in the big picture of our lives—all the things we have discussed in the previous chapters. I believe that God wants us to recognize our magnificence, love ourselves and each other, and laugh compassionately at life. People who have had near death experiences report that their thoughts at that critical near-death time were not focused on all the *stuff* they had accomplished or acquired. Their thoughts were about how well they had loved. Ask yourself how well you love yourself and the other people in your life—your family and friends—and if you encourage the people in your life to be the best they can be. When we are in harmony with others, our lives work; when we are in disharmony, our lives are filled with drama. Choose to be a loving, kind person and watch how easy your life becomes.

The *Prayer of St. Francis* is a Christian prayer by the thirteenth-century Saint Francis of Assisi. It is a prayer that truly touches your heart and soul with positive energy if you allow it to. Take a moment and really *feel* the power of these words: "Lord, make me an instrument of thy peace. Where there is hatred, let me sow love. Where there is injury, pardon. Where there is doubt, faith. Where there is despair, hope. Where there is darkness, light. Where there is sadness, joy. O divine Master, grant that I may not so much seek to be consoled as to console. To be understood as to understand. To be loved as to love. For it is in giving that we receive. It is in pardoning that we are pardoned. It is in dying to self that we are born to eternal life."

Saint Francis did not ask God to fix his life. He asked God to make him an instrument of his peace and love and joy. He asked God to allow him to be as God is so that he could live his life making a difference. He asked God to let him be more concerned with helping others than living his life as though everything was all about him. *Dying to self* is releasing the need to let your ego run your life. When our egos are in charge, our focus is on making other people see life as we do—trying to get other people to agree with us or prove to them that we are right, and that requires a lot of energy. Being *born to eternal life* means you can allow your life to be good now. You can release the needs of your ego and be more concerned with being loving and kind rather than being right all the time—you can live your life being the best person you can be ... right now! Really read these words and feel what it would feel like to be *an instrument of God's peace*. Then go out into your world remembering these words when the challenges come up. By simply shifting your reaction to your world, you can make a difference *and* remain at peace.

The Dalai Lama put it this way, "I feel that my mission is to express my feeling about the importance of kindness and compassion. I practice these things and it gives me more happiness and success. If I practiced anger or jealousy or bitterness, no doubt my smile would disappear."

I can't say it enough. Enjoy this day! Your life is happening right now—this life is not a dress rehearsal. This moment is truly the only one you have, so be unwilling to allow anything but good thoughts in your mind. Take charge of your future, use the tools you have been given in this book. Keep it with you and read it every day. Share it with your friends and make good choices that you can be proud of. Be the person you would like to have as a friend—someone you can count on to be honest, supportive, and kind ... a person with integrity. Live your life that way and you will have more friends than you ever dreamed possible. Remember, people want to be around people who make them feel good—who make their hearts smile.

Just a thought girls (and guys if you're willing)—start a *Heart Smiling* movement. Get some T-shirts printed with a picture of a heart smiling and give them to your friends. You might even add *drama is optional!* That's how easily thoughts can shift and change can take place. Looking at those hearts smiling will be a reminder to be happy, let any *drama* go, and make the *choice* to enjoy your life each day.

And, I want you to know how much I appreciate your reading this book ... you have definitely made *my heart smile!*

978-0-595-42563-1
0-595-42563-1

Printed in the United States
135097LV00005B/5/A